He 111
KAMPFGESCHWADER
ON THE RUSSIAN FRONT

SERIES EDITOR: TONY HOLMES

OSPREY COMBAT AIRCRAFT 100

He 111
KAMPFGESCHWADER
ON THE RUSSIAN FRONT

JOHN WEAL

OSPREY
PUBLISHING

Front Cover
The fourth week of June 1941 saw the Soviet Red Air Force suffer the highest losses ever recorded in the annals of air warfare. On the first day alone – 22 June (the day Hitler launched Operation *Barbarossa,* his invasion of the Soviet Union) – the Russians admitted the loss of 1200 combat aircraft. Some 336 were shot down, with the remainder being destroyed on the ground.

Desperate times called for desperate measures. And no measure was surely more desperate than the Soviet '*taran*' aerial ramming attack. By the close of that fateful 22 June 1941 at least nine such attacks had been carried out against Luftwaffe aircraft. These near suicidal assaults would continue, albeit in ever diminishing numbers, throughout the course of the war. By the end of the conflict it is estimated that almost 600 Luftwaffe machines had been by brought down by '*taran*'.

Mark Postlethwaite's dramatic cover painting graphically captures the moment when a Soviet fighter pilot, his I-16 already damaged and pouring flames and smoke, deliberately slices into the tail of a winter-camouflaged He 111 of KG 53 during a daylight bombing raid 'somewhere in the central sector' late in 1941 (*Cover artwork by Mark Postlethwaite*)

First published in Great Britain in 2013 by Osprey Publishing
Midland House, West Way, Botley, Oxford, OX2 0PH
43-01 21st Street, Suite 220B, Long Island City, NY, 11101, USA

E-mail: info@ospreypublishing.com

Osprey Publishing is part of the Osprey Group

A CIP catalogue record for this book is available from the British Library

ISBN: 978 1 78096 307 5
PDF e-book ISBN: 978 1 78096 308 2
e-Pub ISBN: 978 1 78096 309 9

Edited by Tony Holmes
Cover Artwork by Mark Postlethwaite
Aircraft Profiles by John Weal
Index by Alan Thatcher
Originated by PDQ Digital Media Solutions, UK
Printed in China through Asia Pacific Offset Limited

13 14 15 16 17 10 9 8 7 6 5 4 3 2 1

Osprey Publishing is supporting the Woodland Trust, the UK's leading woodland conservation charity, by funding the dedication of trees.

www.ospreypublishing.com

CONTENTS

OBJECTIVE *MOSKAU*

When German forces invaded Poland on 1 September 1939 an entirely new form of warfare was unleashed upon an unsuspecting world – *Blitzkrieg*. The Wehrmacht's tactics of combining highly mobile, mechanised movement on the ground with close support from the air effectively defeated the Poles in the space of just 18 days.

Eight months were to pass before Hitler launched his next major *Blitzkrieg* campaign. But the Western Allies had failed to heed the lessons of Poland. Theirs was still very much a Great War mentality, their minds dominated by static defences and fixed fields of fire. They frittered away the eight months' grace offered by the 'Phoney War', with the French Army hunkered down behind its Maginot Line and the British Expeditionary Force occupied mainly in pouring concrete and digging trenches. The invasion of France and the Low Countries on 10 May 1940 was thus a virtual re-run of the events in Poland the previous autumn, as the Wehrmacht's armoured spearheads, superbly covered from the air, rampaged seemingly at will deep into the enemy's heartland. Dutch forces surrendered after just five days. The Belgians laid down their arms two weeks later. And exactly four weeks after that a ceasefire signalled the defeat of France.

It would be another full year, 22 June 1941, before Hitler was ready to embark on his most ambitious *Blitzkrieg* of all, codenamed Operation *Barbarossa* – the invasion of the Soviet Union. By then, however, one of the major weapons of the earlier *Blitzkrieg* campaigns no longer featured quite so prominently on the Luftwaffe's order of battle. Despite being described as 'one of the most outstanding warplanes of the mid-1930s', and having formed the backbone of the Luftwaffe's bomber arm during the first 12 months of the war, by 1941 Heinkel's elegant He 111 was steadily being replaced in frontline service by the more modern Junkers Ju 88.

The figures tell the story. For the attack on Poland the Luftwaffe had mustered more than 400 serviceable He 111s. On the eve of the *Blitzkrieg* in the west that number had risen to very nearly 650. But for *Barbarossa* the Luftwaffe fielded just over 200 serviceable Heinkels (well under half the number of Ju 88s ranged against the USSR). Yet although in seeming decline, the He 111 was to enjoy a whole new lease of life on the eastern front, where it would remain in service, albeit in decreasing strength, right up until the very end.

All bar nine of the 215 Heinkels that took part in the opening day of the campaign against the Soviet Union were concentrated in just three *Kampfgeschwader*. But these three units were not deployed equally along the three sectors that made up the main fighting front. In the northern sector, for example, stretching almost the entire length of the East Prussian border up to the Baltic Sea, *Luftflotte* (Air Fleet) 1's line-up included a grand total of just three He 111s, and two of these belonged to a weather-reconnaissance *Staffel*. The northern sector's *sole* He 111 bomber was a

Two He 111s of KG 55 are silhouetted against the lightening sky as they climb away from their field in Poland on the first morning of *Barbarossa*

machine operated by the *Geschwaderstab* of Oberst Karl Angerstein's otherwise Ju 88-equipped KG 1 'Hindenburg'. And as there is no mention in the unit's casualty lists for 1941 of a *Stab* He 111 being lost, it seems likely that the *Kommodore* was persuaded to part with his pet Heinkel for a Ju 88 soon after the start of *Barbarossa*.

Luftflotte 2 in the central sector boasted all of three weather-reconnaissance He 111s. But here in Poland there was also a complete *Geschwader* of He 111 bombers. Forming part of II. *Fliegerkorps*, Oberstleutnant Paul Weitkus' KG 53 'Legion Condor' was based on three fields to the south and southeast of Warsaw – Weitkus' *Stab* and II. *Gruppe* at Radom, I./KG 53 at Grojec and III./KG 53 at Radzyn.

II. *Fliegerkorps* was the more southerly of *Luftflotte* 2's two component *Korps* (the other, General von Richthofen's VIII. *Fliegerkorps* up near Poland's border with East Prussia, did not include any He 111 units).

But on II. *Fliegerkorps'* immediate right, in southern Poland, were the three *Gruppen* of Oberstleutnant Benno Kosch's KG 55 'Greif'. *Stab*, I. and II./KG 55 were all based at Labunie, roughly midway between Lublin and Lemberg (Lvov). III./KG 55 was stationed at nearby Klemensov. KG 55 formed part of V. *Fliegerkorps*, one of the two *Korps* controlled by *Luftflotte* 4 in the southern sector. In addition to its six weather-reconnaissance He 111s, *Luftflotte* 4 was the only air fleet facing the Russians to have two *Kampfgeschwader* of Heinkel bombers under its command. In fact, the bomber element of its IV. *Fliegerkorps* – the southernmost *Korps* on the whole front – was made up entirely of He 111s. All four *Gruppen* were concentrated down in Rumania. Major Gerhard Ullbricht's *Geschwaderstab* KG 27 'Boelcke', with its I. and II. *Gruppen*, occupied Focsani-South, some 200 kilometres from the Black Sea coast, while III./KG 27 was just over 50 kilometres away at Zilistea,

7

A stick of bombs neatly placed in the middle of a group of Polikarpov fighters. Although none of the machines has been destroyed, the proximity of the craters suggests that they may well have been damaged by flying shrapnel and debris. Few Soviet fighters got into the air on the morning of 22 June 1941...

a field it shared with the Heinkels of Major Wolfgang Bühring's II./KG 4 'General Wever'.

These then were the dispositions of the ten He 111 *Kampfgruppen* deployed along the eastern front in preparation for the invasion of the Soviet Union. Launched in the early hours of 22 June 1941, Operation *Barbarossa* would open in true *Blitzkrieg* style with a concerted assault on the enemy's air force, both in the air and on the ground. The main weight of the initial offensive was to be focussed in the central sector, where Army Group Centre's ten Panzer divisions would advance in a series of giant pincer movements along either side of the Minsk-Moscow highway as they drove hard for the Soviet capital.

Before they could do so, however, the Red Air Force had to be neutralised. This was the task assigned to the two *Fliegerkorps* of the central sector's *Luftflotte* 2. Much has been written in the past of the spectacular successes chalked up by the Stukas and fighters of VIII. *Fliegerkorps* in the opening hours and days of *Barbarossa*. But an equally important part in the opening strikes against the Red Air Force was played by the twin-engined bombers of II. *Fliegerkorps*. And those bombers included the He 111s of KG 53.

It had been 18 June 1941 when Oberstleutnant Paul Weitkus' three *Gruppen* – I. and II./KG 53 in northern France and III./KG 53 resting and refitting in Silesia – had suddenly received orders to transfer immediately to the three airfields south of Warsaw. The move to Poland came as a complete surprise, and rumours abounded as to the reasons behind it. Some were even convinced that the Soviets were about to grant the *Geschwader* free passage to Baku, on the Caspian Sea coast, from where their Heinkels would mount a bombing offensive against the British in the Middle East!

The truth was finally revealed on the afternoon of 21 June when the crews were assembled for a preliminary briefing. The experiences of 9./KG 53 at Radzyn were typical. After explaining that extensive aerial reconnaissance had established beyond doubt that the Soviet Union was on the point of launching an unprovoked attack on East Prussia and the *Generalgouvernement* (German-occupied Poland), an unusually serious Hauptmann Fritz Pockrandt, the *Kapitän* of 9. *Staffel*, gave details of III./KG 53's target for the following morning. The *Gruppe's* objective was the Soviet fighter airfield at Bielsk-Pilici, which was located south of Bialystok about 80 kilometres inside enemy territory. Specifically, 9. *Staffel* was to target the field's runway and ammunition dump, leaving 7. *Staffel* to concentrate on the admin buildings and barracks blocks and 8. *Staffel* to bomb the aircraft that reconnaissance had reported as being 'parked in neat rows' along the eastern perimeter of the field.

This news was at first received in something akin to stunned silence. But the crews would have a good seven hours in which to digest and come to terms with the enormity of the task that confronted them – namely all-out war against the Soviet Union – before they gathered for a final briefing at 2300 hrs. Takeoff was scheduled for 0330 hrs the following morning. Aircrews would be woken at 0130 hrs, which did not leave a lot of time for sleep. A 9. *Staffel* NCO takes up the story;

'In the command post the *Gruppenkommandeur* (Major Richard Fabian) goes over the situation one last time, verifies the targets and wishes everyone *'Hals und Beinbruch!'* – 'Good luck!' He will be leading the attack. Each crew is driven out to its aircraft. A large fire is burning somewhere in the far distance and a faint stripe low along the horizon heralds the start of the new day. Out at the aircraft each crew chief reports his machine all ready and fully serviceable.

'A lot of thoughts are going though my head. It's still dark, and this airfield, which we've only occupied for a couple of days and aren't used to yet, is horribly small. Will we be able to take off in our heavily loaded machines?

'We climb into our trusty old crates. A final check to make sure that everything is in order, although it's hardly necessary – we know that we can rely 100 per cent on the work of our groundcrews. The pilot runs up his engines and raises his hand – all set to go! A moment later the three machines of the leading *Kette* start to taxi out, bumping and jolting over the uneven grass surface of the field. Despite their heavy loads, all machines lift off smoothly and safely. Takeoff – 0330 hrs on the dot!

'The *Gruppe* makes a wide climbing turn to the left, gets into formation and heads towards Siedlce to rendezvous with our fighter escort. But the single-engined gentlemen fail to turn up. We are not too worried. We've got machine guns of our own. The formation alters course slightly and sets off for the target. At 0415 hrs we cross the River Bug, which marks the border with Russia. I peer out. A thick mist covers the ground below, but it is not long before the target comes into sight. I'm amazed that there has been no reaction from the enemy yet – he's in for a nasty surprise any moment now.

'Our bombs tumble earthwards. Flashes of flame, clouds of smoke, fountains of dirt and dust mixed with debris of every kind shoot high into the sky. Unluckily, our own bombs just miss the ammunition bunkers we were aiming for, but the stick marches out across the field and causes considerable damage. Two bombs are direct hits

... most being unceremoniously pushed to one side upon the arrival of the advancing ground troops (but only after having their red stars removed by the souvenir-hungry soldiery)

on the runway. No fighters will be taking off from here for a while as the other *Ketten* of our *Staffel* have churned up the entire surface. As we bank away I can see that 15 of the parked enemy fighters are already on fire, as too are many of the barracks blocks.

'Suddenly Toni yells "Flak!" But it's just one solitary burst, and a good kilometre behind us for we are well out of range of the field's defences by now. Then a more alarming message over the intercom – "Fighters approaching from astern!" Our machine guns start to chatter. The formation closes up even tighter. This might mean that we present a bigger target to the enemy, but the concentrated fire from our 27 aircraft is already spraying around the Russians' ears. They don't like this one little bit and immediately dive away.

'The River Bug reappears in front of us. Artillery duels are going on from either bank, but otherwise there are no signs of life below. Soon our base comes into view, and moments later the whole *Gruppe* is safely back on the ground. We have suffered no losses. Reconnaissance shows that we have plastered the target so thoroughly that a planned second strike is called off. Towards evening we are sent up again, this time to attack the airfield at Bialystok, which has already been hit by a number of other units during the course of the day.'

With I. and II./KG 53 also attacking Soviet airfields and installations in the Bialystok region without incurring a single casualty, the *Geschwader's* first day of *Barbarossa* had been a resounding success. But it was a different story on the far side of the Pripyat Marshes – the huge tract of swamp and marshland that roughly separated Army Group Centre from Army Group South – where Oberstleutnant Benno Kosch's *Kampfgeschwader* 55 was to undergo its baptism of fire against the Soviet Union.

The crews of KG 55, like those of KG 53, had been briefed on the afternoon of 21 June. Their targets were a number of airfields in the Kiev Military District, most notably Lemberg (Lvov), which, according to an intelligence report, was also the location of the HQ of Marshal Semyon Budyonny, Commander-in-Chief of the Soviet armed forces of the Southwestern Direction.

By 0300 hrs the next morning, as the eastern sky began to lighten, all crews were aboard their aircraft and the pilots were warming up their

More fragmentation bombs tumble from the bellies of the next wave of attacking He 111s

The crew of a He 111 numbered five. The navigator/bomb-aimer (seen left, holding map) was usually the aircraft commander. Between him and the pilot (right), the wireless-operator/dorsal gunner has come forward from his station aft of the bomb-bay. This rear compartment housed two further gunners, one of whom also doubled as the flight mechanic engines. The *Kommodore* was awaiting a signal from *Fliegerkorps* at Zamosc giving the order to take off. The *Geschwader's* call sign was 'Ostmark' (literally the 'Eastern Marches', the name by which Austria was officially known during its years as part of the Greater German Reich) and each of the *Gruppen* was identified by one of the region's provinces. The order came through within minutes. '"Haudegen" ["Broadsword"] to "Ostmark" – commence takeoff!' At 0305 hours the first three machines of the *Stabskette* KG 55 began to roll. They were quickly followed by the aircraft of I. *Gruppe* ('Tirol'/'Tyrol'), II. *Gruppe* ('Steiermark'/'Styria') and III. *Gruppe* ('Kärnten'/'Carinthia').

KG 55's raids also caught the Russians unawares. At many of the airfields they attacked, crews reported seeing 'enemy aircraft of all kinds lined up in long straight rows as if drawn up for inspection'. The Heinkels inflicted a lot of damage, but they paid a heavy price, losing some ten per cent of their force. Eight aircraft in all failed to return, and many others were damaged by enemy action, landing back at base with dead and wounded on board. II. and III. *Gruppen* lost three aircraft apiece in their raids on the airfields at Lemberg, Adamy, Zalosy, Mlynov and Luck. Most fell victim to Soviet fighters. But it was one of I./KG 55's two losses – the all-NCO crew piloted by Unteroffizier Werner Bähringer – that perhaps warrants special mention.

In the Luftwaffe vernacular of the time, incidentally, an all-NCO crew (one that did not include any officers, that is) was commonly known as a *'Volksbesatzung'*. And the fate of this particular 'people's crew' provides a small footnote in the history of air warfare. They were returning from their raid on Dubno airfield when, at about 0425 hrs, their Heinkel was attacked by a solitary Polikarpov I-16. For some reason – perhaps its guns had jammed or it was already out of ammunition? – the Soviet fighter was unable to bring down the intruder by orthodox means. Undeterred, the Russian pilot deliberately rammed the Heinkel bomber.

Both aircraft crashed. Four of the He 111's crew were seen to bail out of the stricken bomber before it hit the ground and burst into flames. But the action had taken place some 130 kilometres inside enemy territory, and all four remained missing. The bodies of the fifth crewman – gunner Gefreiter Oskar Restemeier, who had probably been killed when the bomber was rammed – and that of the I-16 pilot were both found in the wreckage of their machines.

This was reportedly the very first example of a *'taran'*, or deliberate aerial ramming attack, of the war on the eastern front (for which the I-16 pilot was posthumously decorated as a 'Hero of the Soviet Union'). But it would not be the last. Exact figures for the number of Axis aircraft

Upon approaching the target area, the bomb-aimer would vacate his folding seat alongside the pilot and lie prone in the nose ready for the bombing run. This particular machine is a He 111P, only a handful of which were still in frontline service at the start of *Barbarossa*

brought down during the war by ramming on the eastern front will never be known, and estimates vary wildly from 200+ to nearly 600 (for further details of 'taran' tactics see *Osprey Combat Aircraft 79 – Junkers Ju 88 Kampfgeschwader on the Russian Front*).

The four Heinkel *Kampfgruppen* based in Rumania on the southernmost flank of the front were not as heavily involved in the initial strikes against Soviet airfields, for in addition to targeting a number of Red Air Force bases close to the front, the three *Gruppen* of KG 27 also attacked enemy troop concentrations and supply lines further to the rear. Their targets were situated in a wide arc from Balti, only some 40 kilometres beyond the border, right down to the Black Sea port and major naval base of Odessa.

KG 27's bombers encountered considerable aerial opposition during their longer-range incursions into enemy territory. They suffered a succession of losses, including at least six aircraft shot down or severely damaged on 24 June alone. That same night – in the very early hours of 25 June to be precise – II./KG 27 took off from Focsani-South for a raid on Odessa. Close to the target area the 4. *Staffel* machine commanded by Hauptmann Heinz Wolf gained the dubious distinction of being the first German bomber to fall victim to a nocturnal 'taran' attack when it was rammed by a Soviet MiG-3 fighter.

Incredibly, Oberleutnant Helmut Putz, the pilot of the crippled Heinkel, managed to make a one-engined emergency landing in open country some 50 kilometres to the west of Vygoda. The crew may have got down reasonably safely (details of exactly what injuries they suffered are not known), but they were still a good 130 kilometres inside enemy territory. Then, more incredible still, a fellow 4. *Staffel* pilot landed close by in the pre-dawn light – accounts of the event give the time as 0345 hrs – picked up the stranded crew, took off again and brought them back to Focsani-South.

This incident is well documented, but the following postscript to the story may well be apocryphal. It is said that the Russians dismantled the bomber and loaded it onto a railway wagon to be taken away for evaluation. In the meantime, Hauptmann Wolf had been assigned a new machine. On another mission not long afterwards he came across the very train that was transporting his previous Heinkel to the rear. He attacked it and, in the process, destroyed his own aircraft to prevent it being of any value to the enemy!

Although the main body of KG 27 was based at Focsani-South, III./KG 27 was operating out of Zilistea – a field that also housed the He 111s of II./KG 4. This latter unit specialised in minelaying, and it had been operating from Zilistea for some time. Having played a brief part in the earlier Balkans campaign, the *Gruppe* (minus its 5. *Staffel*) had been transferred from Vienna-Aspern to Rumania on 21 April 1941. At Zilistea it was then tasked with carrying out minelaying operations over the

The extensively glazed nose of the He 111 offered excellent visibility – marred only by the nacelles of those two Junkers Jumo engines – but gave very little protection against flak or frontal fighter attack

A fighter attack of a very different and frightening kind damaged this He 111 of 2./KG 28. It had suffered a *'taran'* mid-air ramming – note the chewed-up starboard wing trailing edge, the bent aerial mast and the propeller slashes at the top of the fin and rudder – and was lucky to make it back to base

eastern Mediterranean and Egypt. During the course of the next seven weeks II./KG 4 mounted at least a dozen such missions – two against Crete, six against Alexandria (Britain's main naval base in Egypt) and four against the Suez Canal. The mining of the Suez Canal involved round trips of close on 2000 kilometres, which had necessitated a refuelling stop on the Italian island of Rhodes.

Now, with the start of *Barbarossa*, II./KG 4 was to put its minelaying expertise to use against a new enemy, and over much shorter distances. Its main targets were the Soviet Black Sea ports of Nikolayev and Sevastopol, only some 450 and 525 kilometres distant from Zilistea, respectively. In just 12 days the *Gruppe* dropped at least 50 mines in and around the approaches to Nikolayev, and well over twice that number in and around Sevastopol, on the Crimea. Intelligence attributed a number of sinkings to the *Gruppe's* minelaying activities, including two destroyers – one of them the 1660-ton *Bystry*, which went down off Sevastopol on 1 July – a depot ship, and a large floating crane. Despite these successes, and in the face of vehement protests from *Luftflotte* 4, II./KG 4 was inexplicably withdrawn from the eastern front on 5 July and returned to its parent *Geschwader* in northern France.

By this time the armoured divisions of Army Group Centre were beginning to bite deep into Russia. The Luftwaffe's initial strikes on the Soviets' forward air bases had effectively destroyed the bulk of the enemy's air power in the immediate area of operations. Faced with little opposition in the air, the He 111s of KG 53 were now being employed almost exclusively in direct support of the advancing ground troops. But the apparent immunity they had enjoyed on the opening day of *Barbarossa* had not lasted long. On 23 June the crew of Hauptmann Otmar Hirschhauer, the *Staffelkapitän* of 3./KG 53, was reported missing. And 24 hours later a Soviet fighter unit that had escaped the wholesale slaughter of 22 June claimed five of the *Geschwader's* He 111s above the fighting to the west of Minsk.

It was in this region that the armoured spearheads of *Panzergruppen* 2 and 3 met on 29 June, completing the gigantic pincer movement that triggered the first of the great encirclement, or 'cauldron', battles on the road to Moscow. By its close on 9 July nearly a third of a million Soviet troops had been taken prisoner, and more than 3000 tanks and almost 2000 artillery pieces had been either destroyed or captured.

The Heinkels of KG 53 were immediately ordered forward to Minsk-Dubinskaya, ready to lend their support to the advance on Smolensk, the next major objective along the Minsk-Moscow highway. But not everyone was happy at the *Geschwader* being employed in the tactical ground-support role, as these comments from one member of the unit illustrate;

'Why on earth aren't we being sent on bombing raids deep into the enemy's hinterland? We just can't understand it! Operations in direct support of the army in the field are totally wrong. It would make much more sense to direct all our efforts against railway stations, airfields, depots, industrial targets and the like, rather than attacking artillery positions, tank assembly areas and bridgeheads close to the front.'

But KG 53 was not the only Heinkel bomber unit being used in this way. South of the Pripyat Marshes the He 111s of KG 55 were likewise supporting the seven armoured divisions of *Panzergruppe* 1 in their advance on Kiev.

Having lost eight of their number attacking airfields on the first day of *Barbarossa*, KG 55's crews were despatched against Soviet troops in the Wlodzimierz-Luck border region 24 hours later. The opposition they faced here came not from Soviet fighters, but from the enemy's flak gunners. Only two aircraft were brought down, but at least seven others returned to base damaged and with dead or wounded on board.

Unlike KG 53, however, KG 55 interspersed its close-support operations with deeper-penetration bombing missions into the enemy's rear areas. On 25 June 5. *Staffel* reported losing a machine to a 'single-engined fighter' during a raid on Kiev airfield, which lay some 500 kilometres inside Soviet territory. Other airfields targeted during the first week of the campaign included Berdichev, which was bombed on at least three separate occasions. The *Geschwader's* Heinkels also attacked enemy troop movements on the Zhitomir-Kiev road, as well as rail targets in the Vinnitsa-Kiev areas.

KG 55 also differed from KG 53 in that it did not immediately move forward hard on the heels of Army Group South's advancing ground units. It would be the latter half of July before the *Geschwader* first touched down on Russian soil. Hauptmann Heinrich Wittmer's III./KG 55 moved up to newly captured Zhitomir, some 120 kilometres southwest of Kiev, on 22 July. It was joined there by the *Geschwader* and I. *Gruppe* within a matter of days. II./KG 55 did not arrive until mid-August, by which time the Heinkel *Kampfgruppen* on the eastern front had finally found their strategic feet with a series of night raids on the Soviet capital, Moscow!

It was on 19 July 1941 that Adolf Hitler had issued his 'War Directive No 33 – Continuation of the War in the East'. Part of this directive decreed that, 'The attack on Moscow by the bomber forces of *Luftflotte* 2, temporarily reinforced by bomber forces from the West, will be carried out as soon as possible in reprisal for the Russian attacks on Bucharest and Helsinki'.

By contrast, 1./KG 53's 'CH', a tarpaulin covering the dorsal gunner's position, appears to have been the victim of an early retaliatory bombing raid by the Red Air Force

The Luftwaffe's chain of command was complex – at times perhaps even chaotic – but when it came to the issuing of orders there was no higher authority than a *Führer* Directive. Consequently, little time was lost in assembling the bomber force required for a Blitz on Moscow. And the greater part of that force would be made up of He 111s. The nucleus was provided by the three *Gruppen* of *Luftflotte* 2's resident KG 53, all now based on the large, but featureless, expanse of Minsk-Dubinskaya. They were reinforced by two *Gruppen* from neighbouring *Luftflotte* 4 when, on 20 July, I. and II./KG 55 – some 35 machines in all – were transferred northwards from Labunie up to Bojary, close to Poland's one-time border with Latvia.

The remaining five *Gruppen* all came from further afield. The three *Gruppen* of KG 4 – including the minelayers of II./KG 4, which had just returned from Rumania only days earlier – were ordered to leave their bases in northern France and transfer forthwith to the far reaches of East Prussia. For security reasons, the crews were told that they were being sent to the Reich's easternmost province for a period of 'rest and recuperation'. The original intention had been to deploy the *Gruppen* on three separate fields, but very few of the bases in the area had the facilities to house an operational *Kampfgruppe*. The *Stab* and all three *Gruppen* of KG 4 therefore took up residence at Königsberg-Prowehren. As a minor point of interest, this was the first time since the outbreak of war nearly two years earlier that the entire *Geschwader* found itself sharing the same airfield.

The last He 111 units to make up the Moscow attack force were the Luftwaffe's two leading pathfinder *Gruppen*, III./KG 26 and KGr.100, which carried out the move from west to east under the temporary command of the short-lived *Stab* KG 28. Both units had their specialised radio-navigational equipment ('X'- and 'Y'-*Geräte* – see *Osprey Combat Aircraft 91 – Heinkel He 111 Kampfgeschwader in the West* for further details) removed from their machines during the course of the transfer, which, in KGr.100's case, took it from Chartres, southwest of Paris, to Terespol, in Poland. Such was the hurried nature of the move that no provision could be made for any ground staff to accompany the 13 Heinkels on the flight to Poland. Nonetheless, although strictly against regulations, every aircraft had its crew chief safely hidden on board prior to takeoff!

The first raid on Moscow was flown on the night of 21/22 July 1941, little more than 48 hours after the *Führer* had issued his directive. But the Soviets had long been expecting the enemy to strike at their capital, and had had a full month since the start of *Barbarossa* in which to strengthen its defences. The attackers would thus find themselves having to negotiate a belt of some 300 searchlights during their approach to the target, before then facing innumerable anti-aircraft batteries and a force of more than

170 defending fighters over and around the city itself.

An NCO of I./KG 53 who was a navigator aboard one of the 195 bombers taking part in the first night raid on *'Klara Zetkin'* – the Luftwaffe's codename for Moscow – described what it was like;

'A Monday afternoon. The crews are stretched out in their tents. The summer sun is burning down on the dusty, bare expanse of Minsk-Dubinskaya. Nobody has the energy to move. Outside, there is nothing but heat, thirst and mosquitoes – our constant companions here. Our two drivers

Taken after the Luftwaffe bombing raids of 1941, this aerial reconnaissance photo of the centre of Moscow – including the near triangular shape of the Kremlin on the left bank of the River Moskva between the two bridges – shows very little signs of damage

have been waiting at the field's single water point for three hours now, but still no sign of the water truck.

'The *Gruppenkommandeur* makes the rounds of the crews' tents to let us know that there will probably be an op later in the day. We remain where we are, each immersed in his own thoughts, until the duty NCO pokes his head through the flap of the tent to announce that we are now at readiness level three. At last there are signs of movement as the crews start to get their things together – parachutes, flying overalls, helmets, flying boots, oxygen masks, maps and pistols, in case we're shot down and have to make our way back on foot.

'I look around me. The faces have grown more serious. Ten minutes later the duty NCO returns, informing us that we have been brought to readiness level two. We all know what this means. Things will start happening in about half-an-hour. The *Staffelkapitän* comes back from the command post and calls the crews together for a briefing – a large-scale night raid on Moscow!

'We are driven out to our machine. The crew chief reports everything is in order and we taxi out to the takeoff point. One last look at our watches and then our heavily laden Heinkel gathers speed down the runway before lifting off into the gathering dusk. We circle the field's radio beacon and then set course eastwards. Following the line of the main highway that runs all the way from Minsk to Moscow, we pass Smolensk and Vyazma. Our specific target is Moscow's major airfield and its neighbouring aircraft factory.

'The sun is sinking behind us. We have crossed the front and are now flying over enemy territory. All our guns are manned and ready to fire at a moment's notice. Five pairs of eyes search the skies for Russian fighters. Not a sign of the enemy, but we are rewarded by the sight of a glorious summer sunset. Gzhatsk slides past below in the gloom. Hidden in the darkness ahead lies Moscow. Several searchlights pierce the night sky like bright needles. The altimeter is showing 1200 metres. At briefing we were told that we would not encounter much opposition. Then the first searchlights surrounding Moscow spring into life and begin to probe the blackness in an agitated fashion. None has found us yet. Their numbers increase the

Yet some damage *had* been done, as witness this radio-photo of a suburban apartment block

closer we get to Moscow. Below me, I can just make out the highway threading through the darkened landscape towards the enemy capital. I count 50-100 searchlights now. The flak is still silent.

'Despite the assurances at briefing about the amount of opposition we could expect to meet, I must admit that this mass of searchlights is slowly beginning to make me uneasy. To be on the safe side we decide to gain a little more height and start to climb at a steady two metres a second. There! What's that ahead of us? An aircraft has been caught in a searchlight beam – a ghostly white moth in the night sky. Within a matter of seconds several more beams latch on to it. Through my glasses I recognise it as a He 111. It's making frantic attempts to escape the searchlights' beams, but to no avail.

'Our pilot pours on the gas and we climb as quickly as possible. Five other machines have now been coned by the countless beams sweeping the skies. By the time we reach Moscow's city edge we are flying at an altitude of 1700 metres. The flak is now firing wildly from all directions. Shells are exploding at every height. A searchlight beam brushes past us momentarily, loses us, returns and holds us fast. We hurriedly pull our dark goggles down over our eyes as the pilot proceeds to hurl the machine about all over the sky in a series of violent manoeuvres. Normal weaving won't get us out of this mess. More than 30 searchlights have homed in on us, turning the night into day.

'The flak is hammering away for all it's worth. Explosions are ripping the sky apart in front of us, above us, to the left and right of us. Our machine doesn't have the usual night camouflage on the undersides of its fuselage and wings. We roundly curse the *Gruppe's* equipment officer for not getting the necessary black paint from Jüterbog in time. We'll be lucky if we get out of this in one piece. We never experienced this much flak over London.

'There is a sudden enormous crash, a brilliant flash of light and the aircraft shudders – we've been hit! I hastily arm the bombs and pull the emergency release. A huge pillar of flame erupts from the ground below us. We dive away to the southwest. The altimeter is unwinding at ten metres per second, the air speed indicator showing 500 kph. The engines are screaming. My ears are ringing. By now we are down to a height of just 300 metres. The searchlights have lost us. We leave Moscow behind us and head southwards. After five minutes we turn west towards Minsk. Slowly, our wounded bird takes us home. We breathe a sigh of relief as we cross the frontline. After a mission lasting almost five hours we land battle-weary but safe back at Minsk-Dubinskaya.'

The two *Gruppen* of KG 55 that had moved up to Bojary despatched 35 Heinkels against Moscow on that first night of 21/22 July. Unlike KG 53, this *Geschwader's* crews had been warned to expect considerable flak and searchlight activity over the target area. Furthermore, as the direct route from Bojary to the Soviet capital would take them over the infamous nest of heavy flak batteries at Dorogobush, they were ordered to fly a dogleg course over Yelnya. But in his desire to be the first to bomb the Kremlin, Oberleutnant Otto-Bernhard Harms, the *Staffelkapitän* of 4./KG 55, reportedly ignored the order, risked the direct route and was shot down.

Following instructions, the other crews got through to Moscow and bombed the Kremlin with some success – or so they claimed. Major Dr Ernst Kühl, the *Gruppenkommandeur* of II./KG 55, even circled 1500 metres above the Kremlin for a good 30 minutes while the raid was in progress. 'I personally took part in the bombing and observed a number of hits in the target area'. But the Heinkels' incendiaries had apparently done little damage, for an intelligence report later stated, 'Photographic reconnaissance shows no evidence of successful attacks on the Kremlin!'

KGr.100's crews at Terespol were also warned of the flak hotspot at Dorogobush and advised to fly a dogleg course to Moscow. Having done so, they were given a warm reception. They reported encountering the first searchlights and flak at least 30 kilometres before reaching the target. Somewhat fancifully, they likened the Soviet capital itself to a 'fire-spitting volcano', with hundreds of light and heavy flak guns and more than 300 searchlights. The defences, they said, were 'comparable to those of London at the height of the night Battle of Britain'.

The three *Gruppen* of KG 4 in East Prussia were the furthest from the target. The flight from Prowehren to Moscow and back totalled more than 2000 kilometres, which was nearing the limit of the He 111's range. KG 4's crews also compared the Soviet capital's defences to those of London. They made special mention too of the height of the barrage balloons over the target, which forced them to scatter their incendiaries from altitudes of 4000 metres and more. Their bombing results were nonetheless adjudged to have been 'remarkably good'.

Despite this official optimism, the majority of those participating in the raid realised only too well that the attacking force's total bomb load of not much more than 200 tons of high explosives and incendiaries would have had little effect on a target the size of Moscow. The Luftwaffe had certainly failed in its declared intention of 'reducing the Kremlin to rubble'. In fact, one foreign observer on the ground dismissed the raid as 'rather aimless'.

Aimless the first raid of the night Blitz on Moscow may well have been, but stemming as it did from a *Führer* directive, the Luftwaffe had no option but to continue with its nocturnal offensive against the Soviet capital. Initially, the attacks were mounted on a nightly

A He 111 of KG 4 that has failed to make it back to East Prussia is inspected by Red Army troops

A formation of He 111s setting out on a daylight mission on the northern sector flies above a solid layer of cloud

basis, although they quickly began to decrease in both strength and frequency until, by mid-September, they had more or less ceased altogether. The Luftwaffe's already thinly stretched bomber force was by then more urgently needed elsewhere.

The scattered and piecemeal nature of the raids meant that the Luftwaffe's losses remained relatively light. On the afternoon following the first attack an announcement by Stalin ended with the words, 'It has been established beyond all doubt that Russian nightfighters and anti-aircraft batteries shot down 22 German bombers'. In fact, only six bombers failed to return. That same night, a second raid – with the attackers' numbers already down from 195 to 115 – resulted in the loss of just two Heinkels, one of them a III./KG 26 pathfinder.

The reduction in numbers among the attacking force was not due solely to battle damage and serviceability problems (although the latter were undoubtedly a significant factor as the bulk of the *Gruppen* rushed in from western Europe had arrived in the east minus their supporting ground staff). Another reason for the Luftwaffe's decline in strength over Moscow was that a number of units were already beginning to be employed against other targets. On 25 July, for example, the minelayers of II./KG 4 had been briefed for, and were preparing to fly, their third mission against the Soviet capital when, at the last moment, they were sent instead to mine the waters around the island of Ösel in the mouth of the Gulf of Riga.

Another *Gruppe* to be diverted away from Moscow on that same 25 July was I./KG 55. Hauptmann Rudolf Kiel's He 111s were given the unenviable task of bombing the flak batteries at Dorogobush that barred the direct route to the capital. They were fortunate to escape with only one loss.

Even luckier was KGr.100, which had not yet sustained a single casualty in its attacks on Moscow, although the crew of *Gruppenkommandeur* Major Helmut Küster had a close call towards the end of July (exact date unknown) when their He 111 was attacked by a Russian nightfighter over the capital and suffered damage to its port engine;

'We quickly descended to 50 metres and started throwing all unnecessary items of equipment overboard in preparation for an emergency landing, but when the machine gradually began to gain height again and got up to an altitude of 400 metres, we had second thoughts. We crossed back over the front to the north of Smolensk and kept going past our base at Terespol. We knew that there were no spare parts for our damaged engine at Terespol, and had therefore decided to head straight for our rear-area workshops at Deblin, situated on the River Vistula south of Warsaw. We finally touched down there after ten hours in the air, handed over our lame bird and telephoned Terespol to send an aircraft to come and collect us.'

INDECISION TIME

By the end of July Soviet resistance in the central sector was hardening. North of the Minsk-Moscow highway a counterattack by the Red Army had retaken the important town of Velikiye Luki just four days after its capture by the Germans. Hitler's hopes of another speedy and successful *Blitzkrieg* campaign were fading fast. His Directive No 34, issued on 30 July, stated that 'the appearance of strong enemy forces on the front of Army Group Centre make it necessary to postpone *for the moment* the objectives laid down in Directive 33'. The *Führer* therefore ordered Army Group Centre to go over to the defensive (ostensibly to give the armoured divisions of *Panzergruppen* 2 and 3 time to recuperate and make good their losses) while the main emphasis was switched to the northern sector, where the offensive aimed at encircling Leningrad was to be continued 'with all means available'.

To this end *Luftflotte* 2 was ordered to transfer a number of its units northwards to help support the troops of Army Group North in their advance on Leningrad. Among them were the three *Gruppen* of KG 4, which moved up from Prowehren, in East Prussia, to Koroye Selo – a field to the south of Lake Peipus, some 300 kilometres southwest of Leningrad – during the first week in August. This made them the first He 111 bombers to serve under *Luftflotte* 1 on the Russian front.

Directive No 34 also stipulated, however, that 'attacks on Moscow will continue'. And the Heinkel *Kampfgruppen* remaining in the central sector complied with the *Führer's* orders to the best of their dwindling ability. A war correspondent aboard one of the Bojary-based bombers of II./KG 55 described an early August raid on the Soviet capital in somewhat vivid, not to say lurid, terms for the benefit of his readers back home;

'By the time we reach Smolensk the clouds are getting thicker and thicker. The Heinkel bomber starts to climb through this bizarre world of mountains in the sky. Like a daring mountaineer attempting an unconquered peak, the machine scales the ghostly white walls towering in front of us – we must soon be getting close to the target area. As usual we are welcomed by fire from the forward batteries some 20 to 25 kilometres before reaching Moscow. Searchlights stretch their long white arms into the night sky. Most of them end in shimmering luminous discs playing restlessly among the banks of clouds.

'"Moscow ahead!" comes the voice of the pilot over the R/T. He points to a break in the clouds in front of the machine. So our "weather frog" (met officer) was right yet again in forecasting good visibility over the target area.

'Just as we are flying through the last wisps of cloud surrounding the dark cauldron that is Moscow, dozens of million-candlepower pillars of light spring into being, casting a net over the enemy's capital. For a fraction of a second a brilliant white light licks the belly of our bomber, but it is unable to hold on to us. Now the city's flak gunners are sending up a curtain of steel. Ignore it! We fly on into the inferno.

Another *Gruppe* of Heinkels – also unfortunately unidentified – approaches its target

'There can't be too many bombers in front of us, for we are part of the first wave. Even so, Moscow has already been hit hard. Three large areas of the city are burning – a result of just the first small percentage of the tens of thousands of high explosive and incendiary bombs that will be raining down during the course of the night. In one of the areas on fire four, six . . . no, eight large infernos are raging. This is where the first heavy bombs have fallen. Direct hits on Moscow's aircraft manufacturing plants and supply depots.

'The two large loops of the River Moskva, which wind into the centre of the city from the southwest, help us to get our bearings. We have pinpointed the Kremlin and are confident that we will soon be able to locate the target assigned to us at this evening's briefing, even in the midst of this witches' cauldron of flak explosions and nervously probing searchlight beams. German bomber crews keep their nerve even under the heaviest fire. They remain calm, identify their target and aim their bombs with precision.

'And so we circle, as barrage balloons flit past us like huge black ghosts and bombs from other aircraft in the night sky around us explode in vivid flashes on the ground, until the commander has our own target fixed firmly in his bombsight. Then it's our turn. The aircraft lurches as our heavy bomb falls away, followed immediately by the load of incendiaries that we add to the havoc and destruction below.'

II./KG 55 flew the last of its 11 raids on Moscow on the night of 10/11 August. Shortly afterwards its temporary attachment to *Luftflotte* 2 came to an end and the *Gruppe* returned to the southern sector, departing Bojary to join the rest of KG 55, which by this time was concentrated at Zhitomir, some 135 kilometres west of Kiev.

Denuded of the Heinkels of KGs 4 and 55 (II./KG 55 had departed Bojary before the end of July), the air offensive against Moscow was now the sole responsibility of *Luftflotte* 2's remaining units. Little is known of the movements of *Stab* KG 28 and/or III./KG 26 at this period, but on 1 August KGr.100, having flown four missions against Moscow from Terespol, was transferred forward to Bobruisk. The *Gruppe* was still suffering badly from the continued absence of its ground staff,

Many airfields occupied by Heinkel units on the eastern front were little more than patches of open grassland

which it had been forced to leave behind in France when it was rushed eastwards. The strength of the *Gruppe* had sunk from its normal complement of 36 machines to just 14, and of those 14 only nine were currently serviceable. KGr.100's Heinkels were also part of the 83-strong bomber force that attacked the Soviet capital on the night of 10/11 August – a mission that cost it yet another He 111.

By this time the Heinkels of KG 53 had also moved deeper into Russia. On 4 August they had vacated Minsk-Dubinskaya and transferred east along the Minsk-Moscow highway to Orscha, some 120 kilometres short of Smolensk. As *Luftflotte* 2's 'resident' He 111 *Geschwader*, KG 53 had the benefit of its full ground organisation. And both air- and groundcrews alike welcomed the change from Dubinskaya – just a featureless expanse of grass dotted with tents – to Orscha, which was a modern Red Air Force base with buildings and facilities that were 'comparable to any permanent pre-war Luftwaffe airfield back in the homeland'.

In its first week at Orscha KG 53 mounted four maximum effort night raids on Moscow in quick succession (also losing one machine in the process), but after the mission of 10/11 August its attacks on the Soviet capital abruptly ceased. For the remainder of August and throughout September the *Geschwader* was engaged almost exclusively by day against enemy railway targets. At first crews concentrated on stations, marshalling yards, sections of track and traffic movements in an arc stretching from Vyazma, through Bryansk and down to Gomel. By the end of September they were attacking the line between Orel and Kursk.

What might be described as the He 111's only sustained (albeit short-lived) strategic bombing offensive of the war against Russia was thus effectively at an end. There would be further raids on Moscow, of course, but not on a nightly basis, and certainly not in the same numbers. Henceforth, the Luftwaffe's eastern front Heinkels would be used more and more in support of the ground fighting. This was not to everyone's liking. 'It was very disappointing', a *Staffelkapitän* of KG 53 would later write, 'to find ourselves flying missions in direct support of the army. It would have made much more sense to be attacking targets such as railway stations, stores depots, airfields, industrial plants and the like far in the enemy's rear. We ought to have cut the Russian front off from its supplies.

'At that time our bomber arm was still a powerful weapon and quite capable of penetrating the enemy's hinterland during daylight. But it didn't happen. The chance was wasted. And so the Russians, who at that stage were clearly still off-balance and reeling from our initial onslaught, were able to stabilise their position and, in the months that followed, even reverse the course of the war in their favour.'

When the *Führer* directive of 30 July, ordering Army Group Centre to go over to the defensive, had been announced, the 'cauldron' battle of Smolensk was nearing its climax. Six days later *Panzergruppen* 2 and 3 had completed their encirclement and smashed the bulk of three Soviet armies. Among the staggering amount of war materiel lost to the Russians were 3205 tanks either captured or destroyed – more than the Germans had on the entire eastern front! It had been during the brief hiatus following the fall of Smolensk, while Guderian's and Hoth's armoured divisions were withdrawn from the frontline for 'quick rehabilitation' as per the *Führer's* instructions, that the Heinkel *Gruppen* – temporarily released from their ground support obligations – mounted the 10/11 August night raid on Moscow.

In the middle of its subsequent seven-week stint attacking the Soviet rail network, KG 53 flew a short series of bombing missions against Red Army troop and artillery positions to the east of Smolensk. A participant in one of these raids, aimed at a mass of Soviet troops hemmed into a pocket some ten kilometres in diameter near Yelnya, described releasing his stick of bombs from a height of 1200 metres and watching the enemy below 'milling about wildly like a disturbed ants' nest'.

Meanwhile, KGr.100 spent the latter half of August attacking a broader range of targets. Its missions included a night raid on Gomel, a dusk attack on the Dorogobush heavy flak batteries, a night harassment raid on Moscow and the bombing of a Soviet airfield near Vyazma. In addition, crews also went after traffic on the enemy's rear-area roads and railways, seriously disrupting the delivery of supplies to the front. On 23 August one crew put a large Russian railway gun out of action by plastering it with their full load of 32 SD 50 semi-armour piercing bombs.

The marshalling yards at Bryansk get yet another pounding from I./KG 53

Early in September both KG 53 and KGr.100 flew a number of longer-range missions (each of some four hours' duration) in support of the developing 'cauldron' battle of Kiev in the southern sector.

By this time Hitler had had another change of mind. Less than three weeks earlier he had stated quite categorically that 'the most important aim to be achieved before the onset of winter is not to capture Moscow, but to seize the Crimea and the industrial and coal regions of the Donetz'. Now, in *Führer* Directive No 35, dated 6 September, he was ordering Army Group Centre to

An impeccable formation of Heinkels sends its bombs tumbling earthwards

return to the offensive 'at the earliest possible moment [end of September] with the aim of destroying the enemy forces to the east of Smolensk by a pincer movement in the general direction of Vyazma'.

The battle for Moscow was apparently on again. As if to celebrate the fact, KGr.100 sent its dozen serviceable Heinkels to attack industrial targets in the Soviet capital on the night of 8/9 September. Despite encountering exceptionally heavy flak, all 12 returned safely to Bobruisk.

For the remainder of September, while the ground forces of Army Group Centre prepared to resume the offensive that it was hoped would take them all the way to Moscow, the He 111s of *Luftflotte* 2 continued their attacks on the enemy's railway network. Returning from one such mission in the Orel region on 28 September, a machine of 1./KGr.100 was badly damaged by a '*taran*' attack and forced to make an emergency landing with two of its crew severely wounded. At the very end of the month KGr.100 then mounted two further night raids on Moscow. Bombing from a height of 8000 metres, crews could not observe the results of their efforts because of low-lying cloud over the target area. And although a lot of enemy nightfighter activity was reported, all aircraft again returned safely.

On 1 October KG 53 transferred forward from Orscha to Shatalovka-East and West, part of a complex of airfields some 55 kilometres south-southeast of Smolensk. From here it was ideally situated to support the ground offensive against Moscow, which was launched just 24 hours later. Operation *Taifun* ('Typhoon'), as the offensive had now been named, initially made good, if not spectacular, progress. At the same time the twin battles of Vyazma and Bryansk, which were fought from 2 to 20 October, ended with the destruction of parts of ten Soviet armies. On the latter date the Soviet government evacuated Moscow for Kuibyshev, and a state of siege was proclaimed in the capital. The German advance, however, was already beginning to lose momentum in the face of stubborn enemy resistance and the deteriorating weather.

The Heinkels of KG 53 were heavily involved in *Taifun* from the outset, at first flying in direct support of the ground forces by attacking Red Army troop and tank concentrations immediately in their path, and then ranging further afield to bomb railway supply lines in the Kaluga and Tula areas to the south of Moscow. But they too were caught completely unawares by the

With a SC 1000 *Hermann* bomb beneath its belly, III./KG 53's 'A1+BT' sits in the early winter sunshine awaiting its next mission . . .

. . . but conditions were soon to get very much worse

unusually early onset of the harsh Russian winter of 1941/42. On 11 October the temperature suddenly plummeted to minus 22 degrees Celsius overnight;

'Shatalovka, which had been a sea of muddy puddles yesterday, was today a sheet of ice. The aircraft engines didn't have sufficient anti-freeze. Radiators and coolant pumps froze solid. The crews froze too – their feet, noses, ears and fingers. It was risky to fly for any length of time at high altitudes, as the machines' heating systems could not compete with the intense cold. Oxygen masks froze. Altitude sickness and frostbite were the results.'

For the first week of *Taifun* KGr.100 attacked a wide range of targets, including traffic on the main Smolensk-Moscow highway, Orel airfield and the enemy rail network as far south as Kursk. Then, on 8 October, crews moved forward from Bobruisk to Sechinskaya. From here they were able to provide more direct support to *Panzergruppe* 3's advance on Moscow. Their first missions from Sechinskaya saw them engaging enemy columns in the Bryansk area. During the latter half of October they mounted several raids on Moscow itself, both by day and by night. Early in November they then reverted briefly to a purely strategic role by twice raiding the large vehicle and tank manufacturing plant at Gorki, some 400 kilometres to the northeast of the Soviet capital.

KGr.100's final mission on the eastern front was an attack on Moscow carried out on 12 November. During the course of the following week the *Gruppe* retired to Hannover-Langenhagen, in Germany, to rest and refit. On 11 December it moved to Märkisch-Friedland, where, four days later, it was re-designated to become I. *Gruppe* of the newly forming *Kampfgeschwader* 100.

The departure of KGr.100 left KG 53 as the sole He 111 bomber presence in the central sector. From Shatalovka its crews were doing all they could to support the ground forces' drive on Moscow, but they were not finding it easy. The worsening weather – heavy snow showers and low clouds – was forcing them to operate at ever-lower altitudes as they attacked enemy troop positions and the railway supply lines. This inevitably led to an increase in casualties. On 23 October the *Geschwader* lost five machines, four of them from III./KG 53 alone, including the *Kapitäne* of both 7. and 9. *Staffeln*.

Hard as the conditions were for the crews of KG 53, they were infinitely worse for the troops on the ground as Russia's oldest and most trusted ally, 'General Winter', tightened his grip;

'The army was screaming for support from the air, but in this sort of weather we were almost powerless. We should have been flying maximum efforts but, truth be told, we were often glad when we were able to get just one machine into the air at the appointed time of takeoff.'

Then, on 5 December, the Red Army launched its counter-offensive;

'There was no longer any question of our flying raids deep into the enemy's hinterland. Attacking the advancing Russians became our top priority.'

There was to be no stopping the Soviet divisions brought in fresh from Siberia, however. They surged forward on skis,

The groundcrews had it the hardest of all. These 'black men' of KG 55 at least have the benefit of a warm-air blower to make working on that port engine a little easier

ponies and horse-drawn sledges, their tanks continuing to advance despite the deep snow. 'We attacked the Russian spearheads and supply columns day after day', one crewmember said, before admitting 'but it was extremely difficult to spot them in their white winter camouflage smocks'.

At Demyansk, some 100,000 German troops were surrounded and cut off. Other, smaller formations struggled to make their way back to the defensive 'winter positions' hurriedly being established further to the rear. And suddenly the crews of KG 53 found themselves faced with an entirely new and unfamiliar task;

'Briefing. A supply mission to drop fuel to an army unit immobilised near Klin, south of Kalinin. Weather, foul. We have to circle for a long time searching for the dropping zone. We finally find it. A whole mass of Panzers and trucks stationary in the snow beneath us. They clearly need fuel urgently, and we drop it as close to them as possible. The Panzers are refuelled and immediately push off in the direction of the "winter position", each towing three or four trucks behind them. A few Panzers are on fire, and these are blown up before the rest leave. The troops wave up at us to express their gratitude. We waggle our wings in reply before turning and sweeping back across the approaching Russians. We strafe

This photograph immediately brings to mind the old adage about 'any landing you can walk away from is a good landing', although the pilot of this machine has not managed to walk very far before needing a cigarette to calm his nerves!

them until the drum magazines of our machine guns are empty. Then we too push off home as fast as we can.'

The writing was clearly on the wall. The Luftwaffe's Heinkels had embarked upon the road to Moscow in classic *Blitzkrieg* fashion by first targeting the enemy's airfields. They had then staged a brief strategic bombing offensive against the Soviet capital, before being called upon to lend their support – with ever increasing frequency – to the German army in the field. Now they were being employed to fly emergency supply missions to save that same army from annihilation.

This aircraft from KG 27 has had its wing and fuselage crosses covered to prevent identification from the air, but the number of bombs piled alongside it would seem to suggest that there is little danger of an enemy air raid

Hitler's hopes of a swift conclusion to the campaign in the east had been dashed. His troops had not – and would not – capture Moscow. But while their attempts to do so had been occupying centre stage, what of the fortunes of the He 111 units on the southern and northern flanks of the nearly 3000 kilometre-long Russian front?

After their brief sojourn at Bojary under the temporary command of *Luftflotte* 2, the Heinkels of I. and II./KG 55 had returned to the southern sector in July and August, respectively. Based initially at Zhitomir, the two *Gruppen* had first operated in support of *Panzergruppe* 1's advance on Kiev. They had then transferred down to Kirovograd at the end of August/beginning of September. From here they continued to participate in the developing 'cauldron' battle of Kiev by patrolling the roads and railways to the east of the Ukrainian capital and bringing much of the enemy's supply traffic to a virtual standstill. One 3. *Staffel* crew alone claimed the destruction of seven railway trains in the course of a single mission.

Even before the Kiev 'cauldron' was eliminated on 26 September (and with it four entire Soviet armies), the He 111s of KG 55 were already being despatched against Kharkov and other industrial targets in the Donetz Basin some 400 kilometres further east. They were also maintaining their attacks on the Soviet rear-area rail network. The tempo of operations was taking its toll, however, and on 30 September I./KG 55 was withdrawn to Vienna-Aspern (and thence to Melun-Villaroche, in France) for three months of rest and recuperation. I. *Gruppe* was immediately replaced by III./KG 55, which arrived at Kirovograd on 1 October fresh from an eight-week re-equipment period at Vienna-Aspern.

II. and III./KG 55 flew a number of long-range missions in the days and weeks that followed. On 6 October they severely damaged the tank manufacturing plant at Kramatorskaya north of Stalino, one of the largest such factories in the Donetz Basin. Before the month was out they also bombed the plant mass-producing the first of the Red Air Force's new Ilyushin Il-2 *Shturmovik* ground attack aircraft, which resulted in the assembly lines being evacuated from Voronezh to Kuibyshev. And they destroyed several vital bridges across the River Don at Rostov with the aid of their new Lotfe 7D bombsights.

Between these longer-range raids the two *Gruppen* continued their campaign against the Soviet rail network, as there was more than 2500 kilometres of track within their radius of operations. Such was the efficiency of the Red Army's engineers that no sooner had one stretch of line been destroyed than it was repaired and traffic was soon flowing again. II. and III./KG 55 were therefore ordered to direct their attacks against the rolling stock itself. This paid better dividends. It is estimated that the two *Gruppen* accounted for no fewer than 222 trains, including 21 ammunition trains and 13 fuel trains, and that 64 locomotives were totally destroyed. The discrepancy between the number of trains and locomotives claimed is partly explained by the fact that, at the first signs of aerial attack, the Soviets would often uncouple the valuable locomotive, which would then make off at full steam, leaving the train to its fate!

This success notwithstanding, as in the central sector, a combination of growing enemy resistance and the onset of winter weather began to sap the Luftwaffe's fighting strength in the south too. On 17 November, after less than seven weeks at Kirovograd, III./KG 55 was ordered back to St André, in France, for a further bout of rest and refitting. It was followed six days later by II./KG 55, which departed Kirovograd on 23 November for Nantes.

While KG 55 had been supporting *Panzergruppe* 1's advance across the northern Ukraine – to Kiev, Kharkov and ultimately Rostov (which would subsequently fall to the Germans on 21 November, only to be retaken by the Russians eight days later) – the southernmost of all the He 111 bomber units, KG 27, had been similarly covering the Axis forces' drive along the Black Sea coast towards Odessa and the Crimea. In addition to lending its support to the ground fighting, KG 27 had also targeted the Soviet Black Sea Fleet. On 18 August, three days after the *Geschwader* had moved forward to Balta, its Heinkels took part in a raid on the major Soviet port and naval base of Odessa that reportedly resulted in the sinking or damaging of more than 30,000 tons of enemy shipping.

Leaving the Rumanians to lay siege to Odessa, which the Russians finally evacuated by sea during the first half of October, KG 27 was next tasked with supporting 11. *Armee's* push down the Perekop Isthmus on to the Crimea. By this time, however, the *Geschwader's* recent operations had reduced it to little more than a third of its original strength, and the month-long campaign to break through the Perekop's formidable defences did little to improve the situation. From late September until the end of October KG 27's Heinkels flew numerous, costly, low-level bombing raids against the Soviet fortifications guarding the only land access to the Crimea.

11. *Armee* finally fought its way through to the Crimea on 27 October, but it would be many more months before the peninsula was fully in German hands. After further operations in support of the ground forces engaged on the Crimea, and advancing along the northern shore of the Sea of Azov, KG 27 was suddenly switched up to Kirovograd to replace the departed KG 55. Newly captured Rostov was being threatened by a strong Soviet counter-offensive, and KG 27 was one of the Luftwaffe units hurriedly sent in to try to stop the Red Army's advance. They were unsuccessful, as the Russians retook Rostov on 29 November. The Heinkels of KG 27 then spent the closing weeks of 1941 covering the German forces' withdrawal to winter positions behind the line of the River Mius.

KG 27 was not the only He 111 unit to operate over the Black Sea during the latter part of 1941. In the autumn the torpedo-bombers of 6./KG 26 had been flown up from the Mediterranean to Buzau, some 80 kilometres north-northeast of the Rumanian capital Bucharest. At first deployed against Soviet shipping running supplies from the

It was in Kherson on 21 November 1941 that Oberst Werner Mölders (currently on a tour of the eastern front in his capacity as *General der Jagdflieger*) accepted the offer of a He 111 from Hauptmann Hans-Henning *Freiherr* von Beust, the *Gruppenkommandeur* of III./KG 27 and an old friend from Spanish Civil War days, to take him back to Berlin to attend the state funeral of Ernst Udet. Mölders (seen centre, with von Beust on the left) never made it to the capital, as Heinkel '1G+BT' (in the background) crashed *en route* the following day

An iced-up Leningrad, with the sea canal to Kronstadt naval base disappearing off to the top right

Caucasus into beleaguered Odessa, the *Staffel* then concentrated its efforts on attacking the vessels sent in to evacuate the port. During the first half of October close on 90,000 civilians and military personnel escaped by sea from Odessa to the Russian-held Crimea. The ships carrying them sailed only at night, and most of 6./KG 26's search missions and torpedo attacks had to be carried out in the half-light of dawn or dusk. Despite these limitations they achieved considerable success. In all, they were credited with some 20,000 tons of enemy shipping sunk between October and December 1941.

In the northern sector there had been no He 111 bomber units at all for the opening six weeks of *Barbarossa*. The first to arrive in the area were the three *Gruppen* of KG 4, which had touched down at Koroye Selo, south of Lake Peipus, on 6 August. They flew their first mission in the north two days later – a daylight attack on Soviet troops in the Slepino region – before embarking upon a succession of nightly missions against the Russian rail network stretching from the Estonian border eastwards to Leningrad. They were also called upon to undertake a number of armed-reconnaissance anti-shipping sweeps and minelaying operations over the Baltic. One such was flown on 29 August – the day German forces captured Estonia's port capital Reval (Tallinn). As at Odessa, the Soviets attempted an evacuation by sea. Among the units sent to attack one 30-ship convoy leaving Reval were nine Heinkels of I./KG 4. Between them they sank three freighters totalling about 6000 tons, set two others on fire and badly damaged a third.

As 18. *Armee* closed in on Leningrad, KG 4's crews inevitably found themselves becoming more and more involved in ground support operations. *Luftflotte* 1 – something of a poor relation in eastern front air fleet terms – was totally lacking in both Stuka and ground-attack units at this time, and the Heinkels of KG 4 had to be used in their stead. As one crewmember pointed out, 'It was a task that the He 111 had not been designed for and which we had not been trained for'.

They were nonetheless successful in their new role, supporting the ground forces in their advance on Schlüsselburg, a port town on the southern tip of Lake Ladoga. Its capture on 8 September effectively cut off Leningrad's land access to the rest of Russia. The fall of Schlüsselburg heralded the start of the attack on Leningrad itself, but the offensive was to be short-lived. Called off after just four days, the city was to be subjected to siege instead. This change of policy had little effect on KG 4. By this time its crews were flying as many as three or four missions a day, supporting their own infantry, bombing specific targets within Leningrad, attacking Soviet positions and lines of supply in the surrounding areas (including shipping on Lake Ladoga) and mining the River Neva. Its He 111s were even used for leaflet dropping!

The tempo of operations soon began to tell on the *Geschwader's* serviceability returns. I./KG 4 had already been sent back to Königsberg-Prowehren early in September for a month's rest and refit. When the *Gruppe* returned to Koroye Selo at the beginning of October it was the turn of II. *Gruppe* to depart for East Prussia (where it would remain until mid-December). And with III./KG 4 simultaneously being transferred down to *Luftflotte* 2 for service on the Moscow front, this left just I. *Gruppe* to continue operations in the Leningrad area.

The bane of Russian front unit identification – the blacked-out markings of this machine engaged in night operations 'somewhere on the northern sector' render it totally anonymous...

Nor were these operations being helped by the rapidly worsening weather. The autumn rains turned Koroye Selo's surface into a quagmire, and I./KG 4 was forced to move – first some 100 kilometres eastwards to Dno and then, on 16 October, back to Pleskau, only 20 kilometres from where it had started! Missions in direct support of the ground forces holding the ring around Leningrad continued unabated as the Soviets strove to break their way through to the encircled city. On 15 November III./KG 4 returned from its six-week deployment to the central sector to join I. *Gruppe* at Pleskau. It did not stay long. After flying just a few operations on the Leningrad front, III./KG 4 handed its remaining machines over to I. *Gruppe* on 22 November and retired by rail to Fassberg, in Germany, for complete re-equipment.

I./KG 4 was once again left to soldier on alone. Although much of the fighting around Leningrad had solidified into a static kind of trench warfare more reminiscent of World War 1, Soviet forces to the east of the city were still making strenuous efforts to break the German stranglehold. Many smaller German units along the Volkhov front found themselves temporarily surrounded and cut off. Now it was I./KG 4's turn to be faced with the new and unfamiliar task of dropping supplies instead of bombs. On more than one occasion during this period I./KG 4's crews were required to undertake a supply flight by day, followed by two bombing raids on Leningrad the same night.

As 1941 drew to a close, one of the final targets for the *Gruppe's* Heinkels were the Soviet truck convoys braving the hazards of the 'ice road' across frozen Lake Ladoga to bring supplies into starving and beleaguered Leningrad.

Far to the north of Leningrad, astride and above the Arctic Circle, another Heinkel *Kampfgruppe* had been waging its own separate war against the Soviet Union. The first of the famous 'Arctic convoys' – a trial run of just seven ships – had been despatched within two months of the start of *Barbarossa*. By the end of 1941 Britain had sent seven more convoys of war materiel to the Russian Arctic ports of Murmansk and Archangelsk. All but two of the 64 merchantmen involved had arrived safely.

In August 1941, in an attempt to disrupt the onward movement of this growing flow of supplies by rail from the northern ports down into the Russian interior, I./KG 26 was transferred from Norway to Kemi, in Finland. From here crews were to attack the Murmansk railway some 200

. . . no such problems here. This is '1H+ML' of 3./KG 26, pictured during its brief deployment to Finland in the late summer of 1941

kilometres to the east. Usually carrying 250 kg bombs, the Heinkels targeted not just strategic sections of the track, but also the supply trains themselves – they reportedly achieved a number of direct hits on both. Although the crews described the long hours they spent flying over the featureless forests of northern Russia as 'far less dangerous than raiding the east coast of England', they nonetheless suffered several casualties from the trains' own defensive flak and from the Soviet fighters that were based on airfields strung at intervals along the line.

In the autumn I./KG 26 was moved up to Banak and Kirkenes, on Norway's Arctic Ocean coast. Its orders now were to mount night raids on Murmansk's harbour installations;

'We took off individually some five minutes apart. Our heavily loaded aircraft bumped laboriously along the corduroy runway slowly gathering speed. We began to wonder if we would ever get into the air. It was our first mission against a Russian port, but we reckoned it would be a lot easier than a similar operation over England. The defences wouldn't be as strong or as concentrated – or so we thought. We couldn't have been more wrong! As we approached the target we were met by a storm of fire that was as bad as anything that London had thrown at us.'

Fortunately, the crews of I./KG 26 only had to endure the primitive conditions of northern Norway, and the attendant perils of raiding Murmansk, for little more than a month before returning to the ordered familiarity of Trondheim and their routine armed reconnaissance sweeps out over the North Atlantic.

The Russian winter of 1941/42 had finally extinguished any lingering hopes that Hitler may still have had of bringing the campaign in the east to a speedy conclusion. His last great *Blitzkrieg* had failed. The war against the Soviet Union would drag on for another three years and more before ending in May 1945 – not in Moscow as he had planned, but in his own capital, Berlin.

That same winter of 1941/42 also heralded the beginning of the end of the He 111's operational career as a bomber on the Russian front. Admittedly, that end was still a long way off, and a few Heinkel *Kampfgruppen* would even soldier on until the dying days of the war in the east, but in ever-decreasing numbers and – with one notable exception – to ever-decreasing effect. Their decline was to be brought about by a combination of circumstances, namely the growing strength and modernity of the Red Air Force, the transfer of some units to the southern and western theatres of war and the re-equipment of others with newer and better types of aircraft.

And even those Heinkel *Gruppen* that *did* remain in action on the eastern front would find themselves becoming more and more involved in the transport role. Continuing a process that had already been set in motion before 1941 was out, the Heinkels' support of the armies in the field during the heady early months of rapid advances and successful 'cauldron' battles would be replaced by supply missions when those same armies became cut off and trapped by the Soviets' inexorable drive westwards.

THE SOVIETS STRIKE BACK

Hitler faced a whole new set of problems in 1942. What were his next moves to be? His troops were clinging grimly to their winter positions along nearly 3000 kilometres of front. Retreat was out of the question, as the *Führer* was pathologically incapable of relinquishing ground once won. Nor could his forces all simply remain where they were. But they had now lost the element of surprise and were no longer strong enough to launch a concerted offensive in all three sectors such as they had done at the start of *Barbarossa*. Hitler therefore decided that the northern and central sectors should stand fast before Leningrad and Moscow, while the main 1942 summer offensive would be launched in the south, towards Stalingrad and the oilfields of the Caucasus.

The *Führer* was not the only one intent on making decisions, however. Stalin, misled by the check to the Germans in front of Moscow late in 1941, believed that the time was already ripe for a general counter-offensive to drive the invaders off Soviet soil. Ignoring the advice of his senior officers, he ordered four separate offensives to be launched, and pressed forward at all costs. Campaigns would be fought in the north to relieve Leningrad, along the boundary between Army Groups North and Centre in an effort to outflank the Germans on the Moscow front, in the Ukraine in an attempt to retake Kharkov and on the eastern tip of the Crimea around Kerch. Three of the four campaigns were total failures, but between them they dominated events on the eastern front throughout the first half of 1942 prior to the Germans' own summer advance on Stalingrad.

In the north, when the Soviet 2nd Shock Army stormed across the frozen River Volkhov into the rear of the German divisions outside Leningrad during the second week of January, the only He 111 *Kampfgruppe* in the area was Major Heinz Alewyn's I./KG 4 at Pleskau-South. Its crews were immediately sent to attack the crossing points, causing 'considerable chaos' among the advancing Russian troops. This northernmost of Stalin's four offensives soon began to run out of steam, and by mid-March it was the bulk of the 2nd Shock Army that was itself surrounded in the so-called 'Volkhov cauldron' roughly midway between Lakes Ladoga and Ilmen.

Although a number of other types (including a single Go 242 transport glider) are also in evidence, there are at least 15 He 111s visible on this busy forward landing ground reportedly pictured early in 1942. The gradual resurgence of Soviet air power would later make such gatherings highly inadvisable – not to say downright dangerous

The growing diversity of the tasks being shouldered by the Heinkel *Kampfgruppen* on the eastern front are well illustrated by these two remarkably similar shots. Here, a machine of KG 27, its bomb-bay doors open, awaits its load of SC 50 bombs, each with four cardboard 'screamers' attached to its tail fins . . .

. . . while on another snow-covered field a French-built Matford truck of the Wehrmacht delivers 250 kg stores containers to a He 111, whose flame exhaust dampers suggest that a night supply drop is in the offing

To the south of Lake Ilmen it was an altogether different story. There, the Soviet counter-offensive bit deeply into the German lines to the northwest of Moscow. Many ground units were forced into making fighting retreats, but others were cut off and surrounded – some only briefly, others for much longer. The two most famous such 'cauldrons' were at Demyansk, 80 kilometres southeast of Lake Ilmen, where the whole of II. *Armeekorps* (nearly 10,000 men in all) was encircled early in February 1942, and at Cholm, 100 kilometres further to the southwest, where 3500 troops, mainly of the 281. *Infanterie-Division*, had been surrounded some two weeks earlier.

The Heinkels of KGs 4 and 53 would be heavily involved in all three cauldron battles throughout much of the coming spring and early summer. On the Volkhov front they attacked enemy units trying to link up with Vlasov's trapped 2nd Shock Army. At Demyansk and Cholm they were employed not only in attacking the enemy forces attempting to eliminate the two German 'cauldrons', but also in supplying their own beleaguered ground troops.

Early in 1942 it had fallen to I./KG 4 alone to oppose the Red Army's northern sector advance across the Volkhov. This was because II./KG 4 had been deployed to Sechinskaya, south of Smolensk, for operations under VIII. *Fliegerkorps* (which had been placed in temporary control of all air operations on the central sector after *Luftflotte* 2's recent transfer to the Mediterranean theatre) and III./KG 4 was back in Germany re-equipping. Already fully engaged against Leningrad, the Soviet counter-offensive stretched I./KG 4's operational capabilities to the very limit.

As previously mentioned, on 22 January enemy forces succeeded in surrounding the bulk of the 281. *Infanterie-Division* at Cholm. Support for the besieged defenders of the town immediately became the *Gruppe's* top priority. Crews were soon flying a constant round of dual-purpose missions, initially dropping supply containers to the German garrison and then remaining overhead to carry out low-level strafing attacks on the enemy units closing in on the Cholm perimeter.

The *Gruppe's* other commitments could not be ignored entirely, however, and towards the end of January I./KG 4 was switched back to the Volkhov area to support a German drive aimed at pinching off the Soviet offensive. One particularly successful mission was flown on the last day of the month when its He 111s bombed the township of Grodino, which contained a transport park that had been filled with close to 300 vehicles and some 1000 Russian troops preparing for a renewed assault. And on 3 February crews mounted their first night raid for many weeks against rear area railway stations being used to bring up fresh enemy reinforcements.

But getting supplies into Cholm remained paramount. Under atrocious conditions – with the cloud base often down to little more

Such were the demands and distances involved on the Russian front that many other He 111 units were formed purely for transport and supply duties. The 'B1' code on this machine serving on the northern sector identifies it as belonging to the transport *Staffel* of I. *Fliegerkorps*

than 100 metres and visibility of less than one kilometre, and in snow showers and thick mists that made the dropping zones difficult to find – the *Gruppe* was putting in several missions a day, delivering ammunition and food to those holding out in the pocket below.

With the situation already critical, it became infinitely worse on 8 February when the Soviets also managed to close the ring around II. *Armeekorps* at Demyansk. The supplying by air of a whole army corps of 100,000 men was a vastly more difficult undertaking. A scratch force of some 15 transport *Gruppen*, many of them equipped with He 111s, was hastily assembled for the purpose, leaving I./KG 4 to continue its supply-dropping flights into the much smaller Cholm. But even this was now proving too much for the depleted *Gruppe* to handle on its own. In mid-February II./KG 4 was, therefore, recalled from the central sector to join forces with I. *Gruppe* at Pleskau-South.

For the rest of that month, and throughout March, I. and II./KG 4 operated without pause, flying up to four missions a day supplying Cholm and supporting the German troops still trying to seal the breach along the Volkhov (Vlasov's 2nd Shock Army was finally surrounded and cut off southwest of Chudovo on 19 March). It is said that during the first three months of 1942 I. *Gruppe* had not had a single day's rest. Of the 18 operational crews that made up the unit at the beginning of the year, only nine now remained.

There was to be no let-up, however. Early in April Hitler ordered the Luftwaffe to destroy the Soviet's heavy naval units berthed in Leningrad and Kronstadt harbours. A force of almost 100 Ju 87s and Ju 88s was assembled to bomb the ships late on the afternoon of 4 April. The Heinkels of I. and II./KG 4 were ordered to lead the attacking force and neutralise the areas' formidable flak defences. This they did to the best of their ability. Five hours later they were back over Leningrad carrying out a night bombing raid of their own, albeit with no tangible results.

Despite this mission, Cholm still remained the focus of the two *Gruppen's* attentions. The spring thaw was beginning to make conditions at Pleskau even more difficult, and it finally forced I. and II./KG 4 to retire to Riga-Spilve. Although this field boasted paved runways, it was twice the distance from Cholm. But the units' problems were not over yet. Riga-Spilve was already grossly overcrowded, and when floods threatened to render it unusable, KG 4's two *Gruppen* were ordered even further back, to Gross-Schiemanen, in East Prussia. From here the round trip to Cholm was close on 1500 kilometres!

Nonetheless, supply flights continued without pause. By now the mass of enemy forces pressing in on the pocket was so great that missions could only be flown by night. Initially, this proved no great handicap – quite the reverse, in fact. The dropping zone was marked by two white lights and the Heinkels, snaking in individually, faced little fire from the ground. Even the machines that had accompanied the supply missions by day to act as flak suppressors were now able to carry stores instead of bombs.

A relief force finally fought its way through to Demyansk at the end of April. The defenders of Cholm had to hold on against unremitting Soviet pressure for another week. Although other units – most notably the transport He 111s of KGr.z.b.V.5 – had played a part in keeping Cholm supplied during its 15-week siege, it was largely KG 4 that the troops of the 281. *Infanterie-Division* had to thank for their survival. This fact was acknowledged by a brief but heartfelt message from the divisional CO sent on 4 May;

'Greetings and thanks to *Kampfgeschwader* 4 "General Wever" and to its *Kommodore*

'Signed, Scherer'.

While I. and II. *Gruppen* had been battling with one of the worst Russian winters on record, Hauptmann Hermann Kühl's III./KG 4 had been under training at Fassberg, in northern Germany. Hearing tales of the harsh conditions being endured and the losses being suffered by their comrades at the front, the crews of III. *Gruppe* were impatient to get back into the fight to help them. During the course of February a steady trickle of brand new Heinkels had been arriving at Fassberg. Then, on 1 March, came the bombshell – the *Gruppe* was being transferred to XI. *Fliegerkorps*! This was the *corps* that controlled all the Luftwaffe's airborne units. It could mean only one thing. III./KG 4 had been earmarked for a completely new role. The crews' suspicions were confirmed when mechanics began fixing towing attachments to their newly delivered He 111s. On 7 March the first Gotha Go 242 transport gliders were flown in to Fassberg.

Glider-tug training began at once, initially under the expert tutelage of KGr.z.b.V.1 at Parchim, and then at Fassberg. By late April the *Gruppe's* crews were deemed proficient enough to *(text continues on page 46)*

Back to the business of bombing. A 'black man' scuttles out of the way as a *'Y-Gerät'*-equipped aircraft of 4./KG 53 runs up its engines prior to takeoff. That single 50 kg bomb seems somewhat lost under the broad expanse of the machine's port wing

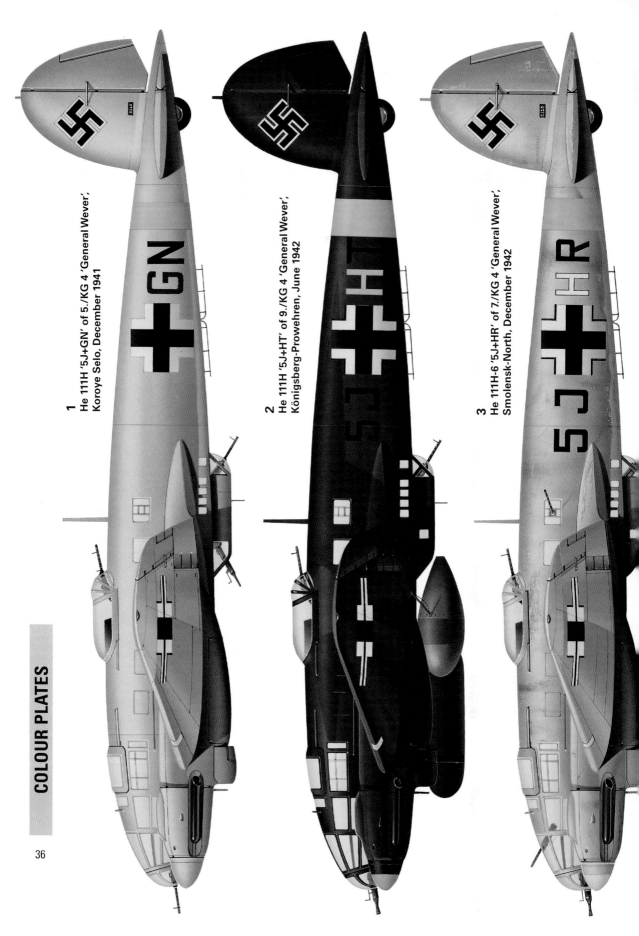

1
He 111H '5J+GN' of 5./KG 4 'General Wever',
Koroye Selo, December 1941

2
He 111H '5J+HT' of 9./KG 4 'General Wever',
Königsberg-Prowehren, June 1942

3
He 111H-6 '5J+HR' of 7./KG 4 'General Wever',
Smolensk-North, December 1942

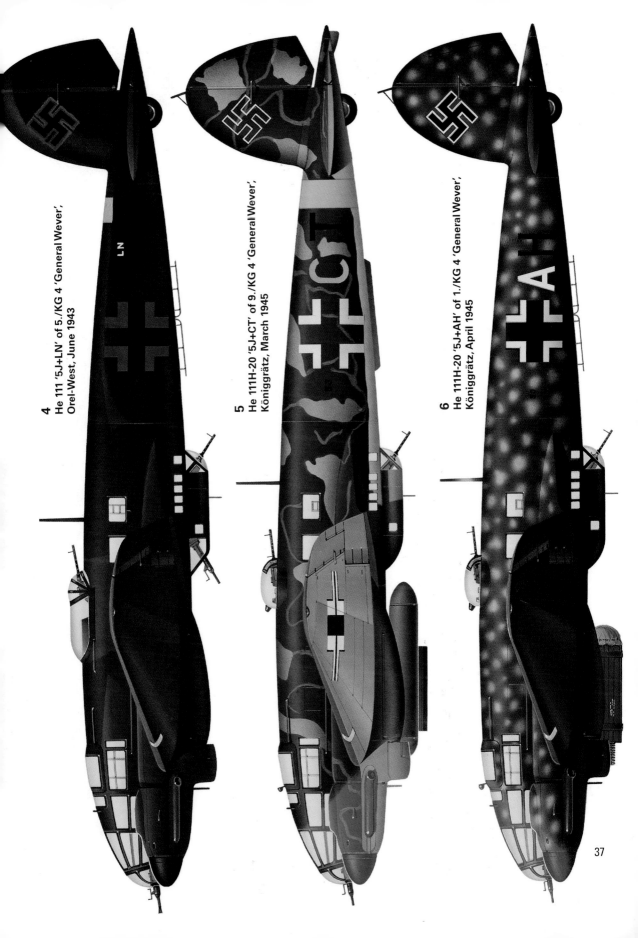

4
He 111 '5J+LN' of 5./KG 4 'General Wever',
Orel-West, June 1943

5
He 111H-20 '5J+CT' of 9./KG 4 'General Wever',
Königgrätz, March 1945

6
He 111H-20 '5J+AH' of 1./KG 4 'General Wever',
Königgrätz, April 1945

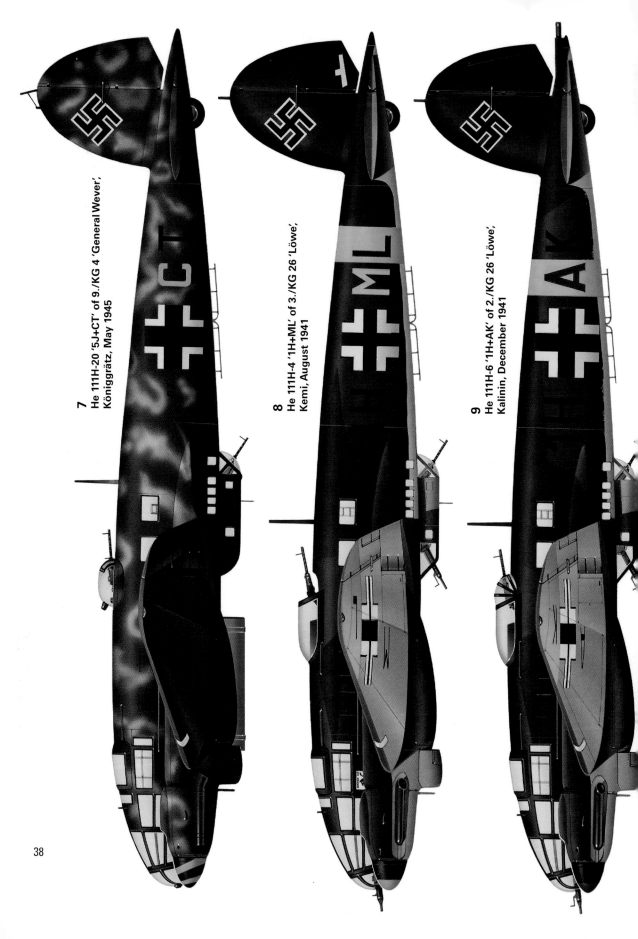

7
He 111H-20 '5J+CT' of 9./KG 4 'General Wever',
Königgrätz, May 1945

8
He 111H-4 '1H+ML' of 3./KG 26 'Löwe',
Kemi, August 1941

9
He 111H-6 '1H+AK' of 2./KG 26 'Löwe',
Kalinin, December 1941

10
He 111H-6 '1G+GP' of 6./KG 27 'Boelcke',
Koroye Selo, March 1942

11
He 111H-6 '1G+FL' of 3./KG 27 'Boelcke'
Stalino, May 1942

12
He 111H-6y '1G+CM' of 4./KG 27 'Boelcke',
Kursk, September 1942

39

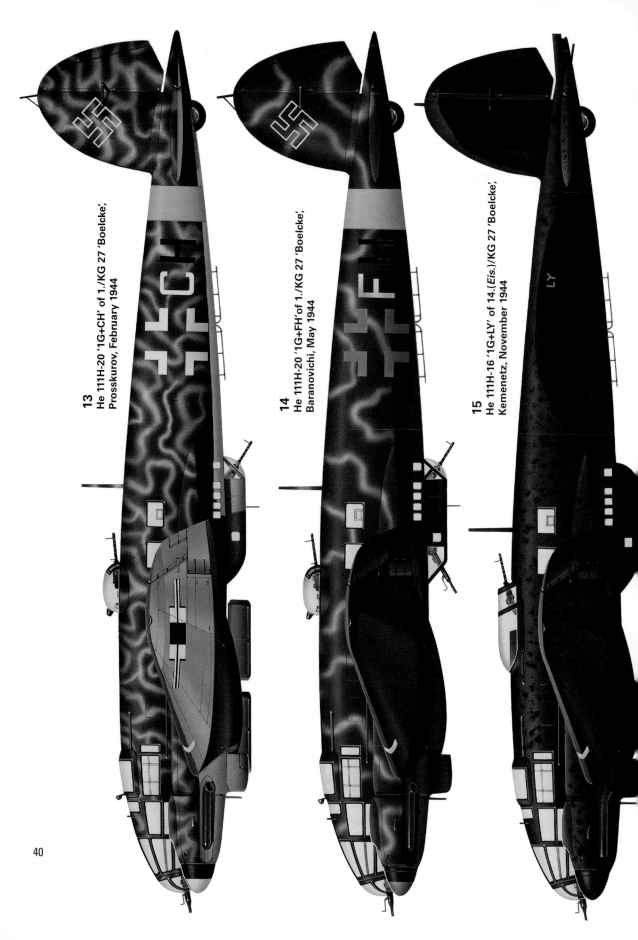

13
He 111H-20 '1G+CH' of 1./KG 27 'Boelcke',
Prosskurov, February 1944

14
He 111H-20 '1G+FH' of 1./KG 27 'Boelcke',
Baranovichi, May 1944

15
He 111H-16 '1G+LY' of 14.(Eis.)/KG 27 'Boelcke',
Kemenetz, November 1944

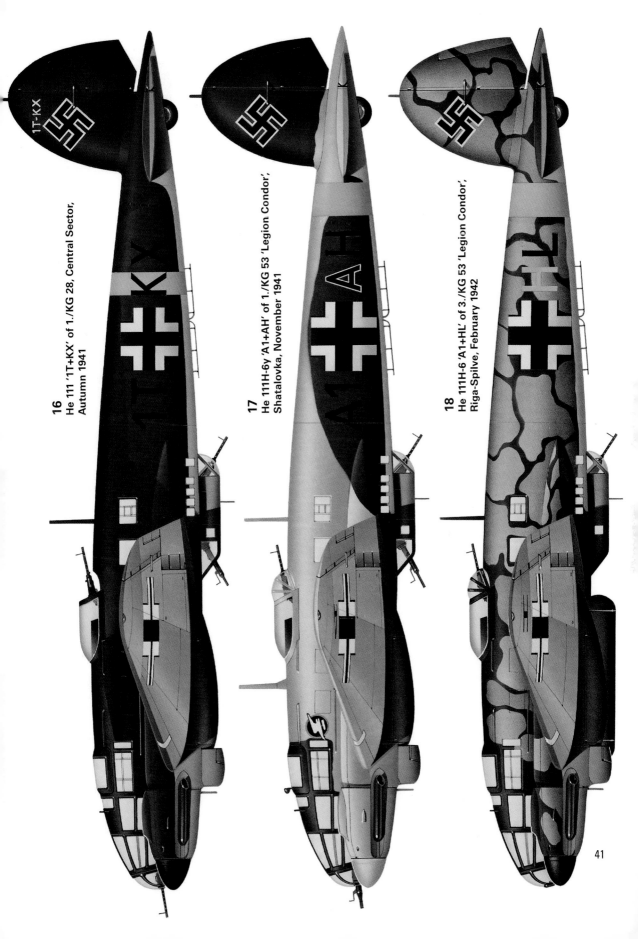

16
He 111 '1T+KX' of 1./KG 28, Central Sector, Autumn 1941

17
He 111H-6y 'A1+AH' of 1./KG 53 'Legion Condor', Shatalovka, November 1941

18
He 111H-6 'A1+HL' of 3./KG 53 'Legion Condor', Riga-Spilve, February 1942

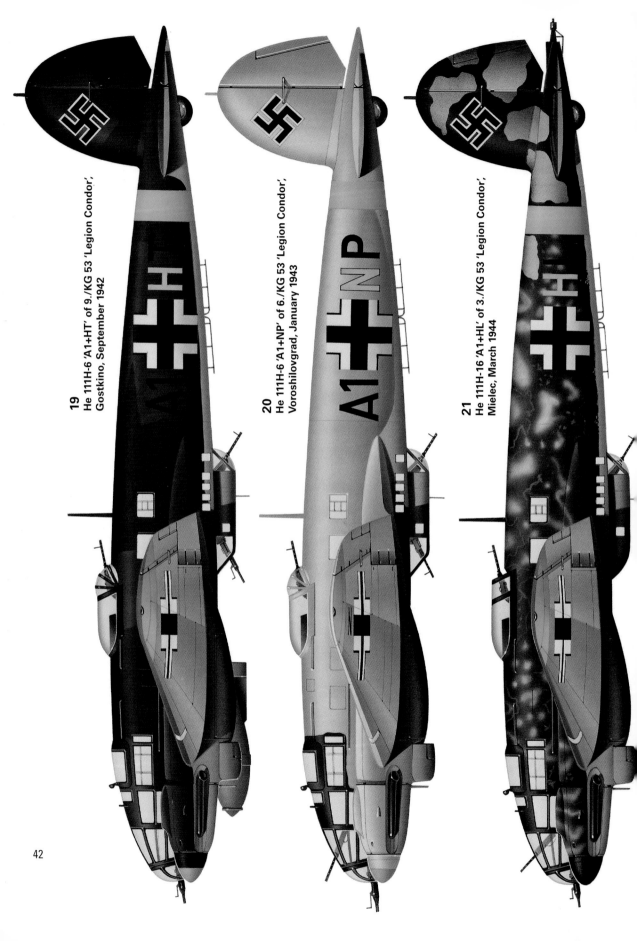

19
He 111H-6 'A1+HT' of 9./KG 53 'Legion Condor',
Gostkino, September 1942

20
He 111H-6 'A1+NP' of 6./KG 53 'Legion Condor',
Voroshilovgrad, January 1943

21
He 111H-16 'A1+HL' of 3./KG 53 'Legion Condor',
Mielec, March 1944

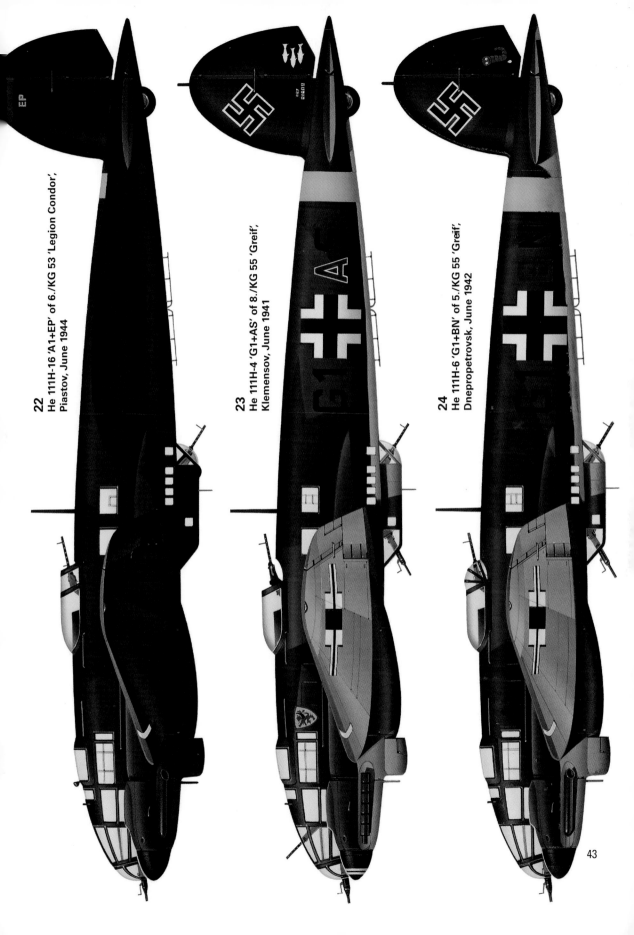

22
He 111H-16 'A1+EP' of 6./KG 53 'Legion Condor', Piastov, June 1944

23
He 111H-4 'G1+AS' of 8./KG 55 'Greif', Klemensov, June 1941

24
He 111H-6 'G1+BN' of 5./KG 55 'Greif', Dnepropetrovsk, June 1942

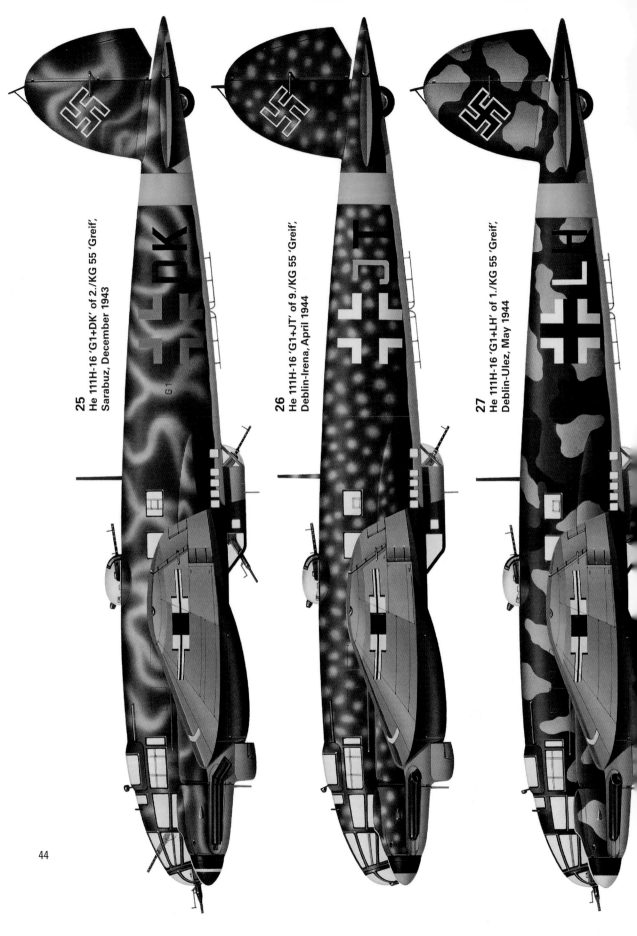

25
He 111H-16 'G1+DK' of 2./KG 55 'Greif',
Sarabuz, December 1943

26
He 111H-16 'G1+JT' of 9./KG 55 'Greif',
Deblin-Irena, April 1944

27
He 111H-16 'G1+LH' of 1./KG 55 'Greif',
Deblin-Ulez, May 1944

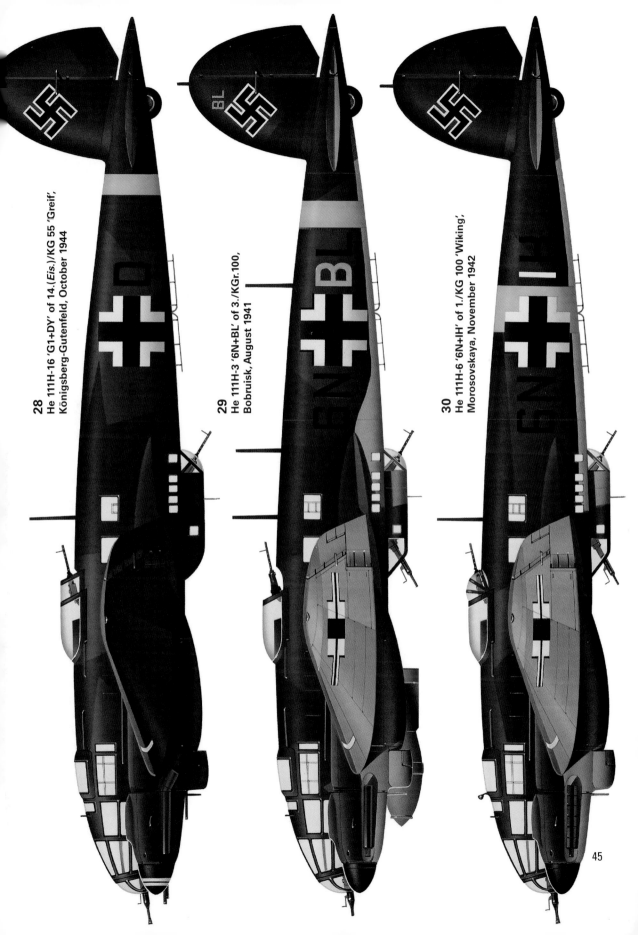

28
He 111H-16 'G1+DY' of 14.(*Eis.*)/KG 55 'Greif',
Königsberg-Gutenfeld, October 1944

29
He 111H-3 '6N+BL' of 3./KGr.100,
Bobruisk, August 1941

30
He 111H-6 '6N+IH' of 1./KG 100 'Wiking',
Morosovskaya, November 1942

commence operations, but there was a delay in the provision of pilots for the Go 242s. Then came another about-face. While 8./KG 4 was to continue with its glider training, 7. and 9. *Staffeln* were ordered to prepare for minelaying operations over the Gulf of Finland. To this end they moved back up to Königsberg-Prowehren on 5 May.

I. and II./KG 4 were already in East Prussia. Their Cholm supply flights now successfully concluded, they too were on standby for the forthcoming minelaying campaign. Although the 4 April attacks on the enemy battleships and cruisers berthed in Leningrad and Kronstadt harbours had inflicted considerable damage, the Soviet Baltic Fleet was far from destroyed. The object of Operation *Froschlaich* ('Frogspawn'), therefore, was to sew a thick belt of mines between Kotlin Island – the location of the Kronstadt naval base – and the mainland to either side of it in order to keep the Russian vessels bottled up in Leningrad and the easternmost recesses of the Gulf of Finland.

A trio of glider-towing He 111s on what is clearly a training exercise. On actual supply operations the Go 242s rarely held station as neatly as this

The first Heinkels took off from Königsberg for the long 800-kilometre haul to Kronstadt late on 27 May. Heavily laden with fuel and mines, they had to use jettisonable underwing rocket packs – commonly known as *Krafteier* ('power eggs') – to help them get off the ground. Despite intense enemy flak, searchlight and nightfighter activity, crews laid the mines successfully and all aircraft returned safely. Operation *Froschlaich* would last very nearly three weeks, during which time the He 111s of KG 4 flew a total of 11 missions to Kronstadt.

In mid-June, their minelaying completed, 7. and 9. *Staffeln* were ordered back to Fassberg to resume their interrupted glider-tug training, while I. and II./KG 4 were rushed down to Sechinskaya, southwest of Smolensk, to support the hard-pressed troops of Army Group Centre.

But if KG 4's services were that urgently required west of Moscow, where was KG 53, which had been the central sector's 'resident' He 111 *Kampfgeschwader* at the start of the campaign against Russia? Like KG 4 to the north, KG 53 had spent much of the first half of 1942 only two-*Gruppen* strong. Late in January the badly mauled III./KG 53 had been withdrawn from the eastern front and returned to Ansbach to rest and re-equip. It would remain in Germany for very nearly six months, being based for half that time at Anklam in Pomerania, where crews familiarised themselves with the new Lotfe 7D bombsight, which allowed ordnance to be dropped with remarkable accuracy from heights of between 4000-7000 metres. Declared operational again in July, III./KG 53 was first sent to France for three weeks to carry out several costly night raids over the United Kingdom – the *Gruppe* losing its newly appointed *Gruppenkommandeur* in the process – before finally returning to Russia in mid-August.

Meanwhile, with II./KG 53 remaining in the central sector, based primarily at Shatalovka near Smolensk and operating over the Rzhev-Tula regions to the west and south of Moscow, I./KG 53 had been despatched to the northern sector to assist in the Demyansk and Cholm supply flights and to help counter the Soviet offensive across the Volkhov. It too lost a relatively new *Gruppenkommandeur* when Major Joachim Wienholtz failed to return from a bombing raid on Vlasov's encircled 2nd Shock Army on 30 March 1942.

By far the greater part of the crews' time, however, was spent flying supplies into Demyansk and Cholm. 'Low-level missions in atrocious weather conditions, by day and by night, loaded with supply containers of every conceivable kind – that was our daily bread', as one participant observed of the *Gruppe's* activities during this period. The unit suffered surprisingly few total losses, but a number of crew members were killed or wounded and many aircraft were damaged by light flak and enemy ground fire.

After the spring thaw I./KG 53 was transferred forward from Riga-Spilve to Koroye Selo. It was joined there in May by II./KG 53, up from Shatalovka, and both *Gruppen* then took part in the final destruction of the 2nd Shock Army pocket west of the Volkhov. II./KG 53 even formed its own nightfighter *Schwarm* of four He 111s, manned by those crews most experienced in blind-flying, to hunt the Soviet transport aircraft that were desperately trying to supply Vlasov's men under cover of darkness.

Once the Volkhov front had been stabilised, I./KG 53 was immediately on the move again – this time to a field closer to Leningrad. Contrary to the crews' expectations, they were not required to resume the bombing offensive against the city. Instead, they were now tasked with preventing Soviet submarines from slipping out into the central Baltic (a sea area that was criss-crossed by German supply convoy routes and also used by the Kriegsmarine as a training ground for its own U-boat crews). In the opinion of most of those involved, this was a total waste of time and resources for an experienced bomber unit that could be far better employed elsewhere. Yet despite the crews' protestations they were to spend weeks patrolling the Gulf of Finland, without achieving the slightest success. Most missions were flown by just two or three aircraft at a time, and nearly all ended in the same way – with them dumping their bombs on the alternative target, a luckless Soviet fighter airfield on the island of Lavasaari.

In the meantime II./KG 53 had stayed put at Koroye Selo, where, apart from a brief return to the central sector early in August, it would remain for much of the rest of the year.

Despite all the to-ing and fro-ing by the Heinkel *Kampfgruppen*, most of the aerial activity in the northern and central sectors – demanding as it may have been – had, in effect, consisted of little more than a series of holding actions. The main focus of operations in 1942 was to be in the south, supporting the advance on Stalingrad and the drive down into the Caucasus. But Hitler's offensive was planned for the summer. And first there were Stalin's two major counter-attacks, at Kharkov and in the Crimea, to be dealt with.

The Soviets' ill-fated advance across the Volkhov in the north had cost them Vlasov's 2nd Shock Army. Their attempt to encircle and retake Kharkov, a major transport and industrial centre in the Ukraine, was to end in a defeat of even more catastrophic proportions. On 12 May the Russians had started to push 600 tanks into a salient on the west bank of the River Donetz to the south of Kharkov just as German forces were preparing to eliminate it. The two sides clashed. The Soviet generals proposed a withdrawal from their dangerously exposed position, but they were overruled by Stalin, who ordered them to stand fast where they were. As a result, the entire Russian front around Kharkov collapsed. More than 1000 tanks were lost and nearly a quarter of a million Red Army troops were captured. One historian has called this battle 'a disaster as great as those of 1941'. The defeat south of Kharkov would prove to be the last such major reversal suffered by the Soviets in their four-year battle against the German invaders, however.

The Heinkels of KG 55, which had supported the advance on Kharkov the

In an effort to protect themselves against attacks from a resurgent Red Air Force, a number of He 111s were fitted with a rearward-firing MG 17 machine gun in the tail cone. The experiment was not a great success, however

previous autumn, were conspicuous by their absence from the area during the first quarter of 1942. The entire *Geschwader* had been withdrawn from operations towards the end of 1941 and sent back to France for a protracted period of rest and retraining. As the first to retire from the eastern front (on 1 October 1941), Major Rudolf Kiel's I./KG 55 was the first *Gruppe* to return. Its aircraft touched down back at Kirovograd on the first day of the New Year after an absence of exactly three months, and they would spend the opening weeks of 1942 operating on the Donetz front from both Kirovograd and Konotop.

It was during this same period that the Soviet forces that had landed on the Kerch Peninsula (the easternmost tip of the Crimea) at the end of December 1941 attempted to mount a counter-offensive aimed at pushing the Germans back off the Crimea. Hitler could not allow this to happen. The Crimea was a vital springboard for his projected advance down into the Caucasus, and Kerch had to be recaptured before this could take place.

Among the units drawn into the battle to clear the Crimea once and for all was I./KG 55. Its Heinkels not only attacked the Soviet troops clinging on to the Kerch Peninsula, but also ranged further afield, bombing the ports along the Caucasian Black Sea coast that were keeping them supplied. In one such raid, flown against Tuapse on 10 April, the *Gruppe* damaged both the 15,000-ton cruiser *Frunze* (which had been towed incomplete from the yards at Nikolayev at the start of *Barbarossa* to prevent it falling into German hands) and the modern 2250-ton destroyer *Sposobry*.

Nor was there a lot that could be done about the increasing number of enemy air raids on the Luftwaffe's airfields. The victim of low-flying Ilyushin Il-2 *Shturmoviks*, this is one He 111 whose operational career is well and truly over

Exactly a fortnight later the remainder of KG 55 began arriving back in Russia after more than five(!) months of re-equipping and retraining in the west. The *Stab* and III. *Gruppe* first flew in to Konotop, but within days they had been ordered south to join I./KG 55 at Sarabuz, on the Crimea. II. *Gruppe's* initial destination was Dniepropetrovsk, in the Ukraine.

KG 55's Heinkels were just a part of the large Luftwaffe force assembled to support German ground troops in a

Yet the Heinkels kept flying. This unnamed trio from 3./KG 53 celebrate their 600th combat mission garlanded in oak leaves and clutching a tasty looking cake apiece...

...but it should be remembered that it was the untiring work of the groundcrews that kept the aircraft serviceable and enabled the aircrews to enjoy their moments of glory. Note the *Kutonase* anti-balloon strake around the nose of both of these machines, as well as the forward-firing 20 mm MG FF cannon and exhaust flame dampers

local, but all-out, offensive to drive the Soviets off the Crimea and back across the Kerch Straits. The Russians resisted fiercely, both on the ground and in the air. A measure of their desperation may be gauged from the fact that on 8 May (the first day of the operation) a machine of 1. *Staffel* fell victim to a '*taran*' attack. Forty-eight hours later the *Geschwader* lost no fewer than eight of its aircraft to ground fire while strafing the mass of enemy troops already beginning to retreat eastwards towards the Straits.

By 21 May all of the Crimea was in German hands (with the exception of the besieged fortress of Sevastopol to the southwest, which would hold out until July). The successful clearing of the eastern Crimea marked the end of the third of the four abortive counter-offensives launched by Stalin in late 1941/early 1942. And the fourth, and greatest, disaster of all for the Soviet dictator was even now moving towards its climax to the south of Kharkov.

When the Russians had first launched their offensive to retake Kharkov on 12 May, the Luftwaffe, fully committed over the Crimea, had little to put into the air against them. But units were quickly moved into the area to restore the situation. Among the first were I. and III./KG 55, which departed Sarabuz on 15 and 13 May, respectively, the former heading for Stalino and the latter joining II. *Gruppe* at Dniepropetrovsk.

From these two fields, some 140 and 200 kilometres south of the Soviet salient threatening Kharkov, KG 55's Heinkels immediately began to make their presence felt. They attacked Russian reinforcements pouring in along the roads from the Kupyansk railhead to the east, dropped supplies to a German Panzer unit trapped in a wood near Ternovaya and distributed 'thousands of leaflets over Soviet and Rumanian troops urging surrender and steadfastness, respectively!'

Although effective, KG 55's intervention cost it dearly. While the Luftwaffe had been concentrating on the Crimea, the Soviets had been able to establish local air superiority over the Kharkov front. It was not uncommon for a single *Kette* of three He 111s to be set upon by 20-30 Russian fighters. And at night, when sent to bomb the major railway stations such as those at Rossosh and Volchansk, which were being used to keep the Soviet offensive supplied, KG 55's crews had to run the gauntlet of massed flak defences.

Operation *Fridericus*, the German counter-attack aimed at pinching off the Soviet salient on the west bank of the Donetz, was launched on the morning of 17 May. The Russians were quickly overwhelmed and soon reduced to just a small pocket of resistance. Next came *Fridericus II*, which was intended to take 1. *Panzerarmee* across the Donetz to capture the strategically important towns of Kupyansk and Izyum, and thus bring it into its starting position for Hitler's main summer offensive. *Fridericus II* was scheduled to begin on 17 June, but heavy rains delayed it for five days.

KG 55 continued to support the ground operations throughout, both directly and indirectly. One 9. *Staffel* crew scored a spectacular success on the opening day of the offensive when their 1000 kg bomb totally destroyed the road bridge over the River Oskol at Kupyansk, effectively severing the Soviets' main line of supply.

The *Geschwader* may have begun *Fridericus II* on a high note, but the battle ended sourly when two 8. *Staffel* machines were shot down in error by German Bf 109 fighters over Volchansk on 27 June. These were the last of the nearly 30 crews lost to KG 55 since its arrival back from France just two months earlier. In that time the unit's Heinkels had played a major part both in clearing the Crimea and removing the enemy threat to Kharkov. The roads down into the Caucasus and eastwards to Stalingrad were now open.

A pair of cannon-armed He 111s of 1./KG 27 – '1G+GK' in the foreground – head east intent on causing trouble

Before following those two roads, however – the one leading to reversal and headlong retreat, the other to encirclement and annihilation – mention ought perhaps to be made of the activities, mainly anti-shipping, of the He 111 units on the southernmost and northernmost extremities of the Russian front during the first half of 1942.

As the most southerly of all the He 111 *Kampfgeschwader* engaged against the Soviet Union, KG 27 was inevitably called upon to fly numerous missions over the Black Sea, targeting both enemy shipping and the many ports along the Crimean and Caucasian coastlines. These operations fell almost exclusively to Kherson-based III./KG 27, which, in mid-January 1942, had been incorporated into the newly created *Sonderstab Krim* (Special Staff Crimea). This command had been formed specifically to support 11. *Armee's* final drive to push the Soviets off the eastern tip of the Crimea and back across the Kerch Straits to the Kuban. Its main tasks were threefold – to carry out armed reconnaissance sweeps of the Black Sea around the Crimea, to disrupt the movement of troops and supplies on to the Crimea and to attack the enemy forces still clinging to the eastern tip of the peninsula around Kerch.

While III. *Gruppe* was thus fully occupied to the south, I./KG 27 had been based at Kirovograd supporting the ground fighting in the Kharkov region. And when, in February, the Soviet offensive across the Donetz began to assume crisis proportions, elements of the *Sonderstab Krim* – including III./KG 27 – were hurriedly transferred northwards to help counter the growing threat. Operating out of Kirovograd-North, III. *Gruppe* would spend the next two months concentrating much of its efforts against the Soviet salient at Izyum, south of Kharkov, before returning to Kherson on 19 April.

It was also in February that II./KG 27 had arrived back on the eastern front after several weeks re-equipping at Hannover-Langenhagen. Rather than rejoining the rest of the *Geschwader* in the Ukraine, however, II. *Gruppe* had been directed to *Luftflotte* 1 on the northern sector. Based at Koroye Selo, crews immediately found themselves involved in the Demyansk and Cholm supply operations. They also flew missions against Leningrad and over the Volkhov front. Whether dropping supply

The evening sun casts long shadows as an impressive line-up of snow-camouflaged machines of II./KG 27 are readied for the coming night's mission. This photo was reportedly taken at Koroye Selo in early March 1942 . . .

. . . but by the following month the temporary white winter camouflage had disappeared. April 1942, and 5./KG 27's '1G+KN' is setting out for another strike on the Soviets' northern sector rail network

containers or bombs, II./KG 27's brief spell at Koroye Selo was to prove costly. One of the three Heinkels that failed to return from a supply flight to Cholm on 6 April actually forced landed inside the pocket. The radio was promptly removed from the machine and used to guide in further supply drops. By early May the *Gruppe* was so reduced in strength that it had to return to Germany for further re-equipment.

By this time I. and III./KG 27 were busily engaged both on the Kharkov front and in bombing the enemy's Black Sea ports. During the course of March III. *Gruppe* had suffered a number of casualties while carrying out night raids on Novorossisk. And on 30 March 1. *Staffel* lost two machines to Soviet fighters over the harbour at Kerch. Then, on 22 April, the crews of 3. *Staffel* were briefed to attack a new target – Stalingrad.

'It was on this date that the name Stalingrad really took on a meaning for me', one crewman of 3./KG 27 was later to write. 'The 900-kilometre approach flight was an experience in itself. Seemingly completely alone, we flew on for hours through the bright moonlit night – the sky above us a canopy of glittering stars, the ground below hidden by a solid layer of cloud. Shortly before the Volga the cloud began to break up. The prominent bend in the river to the south of the city enabled us to get our bearings. We gained a little more height over the eastern bank and then turned in across an island in the middle of the river – another good navigational aid – towards our assigned target, a tractor and armaments factory.

'Even without the clear conditions, the city would have been easy to find. Its position was betrayed by the heavy flak being directed against the aircraft attacking at intervals ahead of us, and by the 50 or so searchlights waving about all over the sky.

'The old trick of making our bombing run as quietly as possible with both engines throttled right back and revs desynchronised worked a treat. This upset the enemy's listening devices and we weren't bothered by either flak or searchlights. We bombed from an altitude of 5000 metres, which gave us plenty of height to dive away as soon as our bombs had gone. After a flight of six-and-a-half hours we landed safely back at Kirovograd.'

By early May I. and III./KG 27 were both down at Kherson again and preparing to support Operation

Meanwhile, far to the south, the He 111s of the Crimea-based I./KG 100 were proving to be a real thorn in the side of the enemy, flying every kind of mission from low-level strafing attacks on Soviet ground troops . . .

Trappenjagd ('Bustard Hunt'), the final push to drive the last of the Soviet forces dug in on the easternmost tip of the Crimea back across the Kerch Straits. *Trappenjagd* was concluded in just ten days, from 8 to 17 May, whereupon the two *Gruppen* were immediately moved back up to Kharkov and Stalino to lend their full weight – more precisely, all 34 of their then serviceable He 111s – to *Fridericus*. By the first week of June, with Stalin's two southern sector counter-offensives effectively smashed and Hitler's own 1942 summer offensive now only days away, I. and III./KG 27 had been transferred to Poltava, roughly midway between the Dnieper and the Donetz, where they were joined on 10 June by II. *Gruppe*, newly returned from Germany.

While KG 27's strength was divided between the northern and southern sectors for much of the first half of 1942, there was one *Gruppe* that had remained firmly in the Crimea throughout that time, and which had been engaged mainly in anti-shipping operations. KGr.100 had been withdrawn from the central sector in November 1941. Now, two months later, it was back on the eastern front under its new guise as I./KG 100. The *Gruppe's* 28 Heinkels touched down at Focsani, in Rumania, on 12 January 1942. From here they mounted their first armed sweeps over the Black Sea, before being moved up to Kirovograd, in the Ukraine, ten days later. Then, on 30 January, the *Gruppe* was suddenly ordered to Saki, on the Crimean Peninsula itself. Initially, Saki was intended to serve simply as a jumping-off point for the unit's Black Sea anti-shipping operations, but the *Gruppe* would remain here for more than six months.

Crews soon had their hands full attacking the enemy's shipping and Black Sea ports, bombing the 'ice-road' across the Kerch Straits and strafing Soviet troops dug in on the eastern Crimea. Their activities were clearly more than a mere irritant to the Russians, for between 18 February and 1 March the enemy bombed Saki no fewer than 20 times. The airfield was also shelled by the Soviet cruiser *Krasny Krim* on 22 February. These bombardments from air and sea resulted in the loss of just one He 111, but 17 others were damaged to varying degrees – three so badly that they had to be sent away for repair.

... to high-altitude bombing raids on Sevastopol, where they employed the ultra-heavy SC 2500 *Max* (which weighed in at nearly two-and-a-half tons) against the harbour city's outer fortifications

I./KG 100's missions continued unabated throughout the enemy's retaliatory strikes. Arguably the most successful of the *Gruppe's* crews was that headed by future Oak Leaves-winner Oberleutnant Hansgeorg Bätcher, currently the *Kapitän* of 1. *Staffel*. On 20 February Bätcher sank a 2000-ton freighter making for Sevastopol. A few nights later he attacked Kerch harbour, where he finished off a 7500-ton tanker that he had first damaged on 6 February. According to one source, the loss of this one tanker resulted in fuel supplies to the Soviet troops on the Crimea being disrupted for five days.

On 5 March the now Hauptmann Bätcher attacked an enemy submarine with five SD 50 bombs while flying an armed reconnaissance mission, but he was only able to claim it as damaged. Three days later another of the *Gruppe's* crews had more success, sinking a Soviet submarine (reportedly the *Shch.213*) south of Yalta.

The Russian counter-offensive that was intended to drive the German 11. *Armee* off the Crimea was launched on 13 March. Although it was brought to a standstill after a week, the areas around Kerch – and around besieged Sevastopol to the southwest – became the focal points for most of I./KG 100's operations for the next three months. Throughout the remainder of March, all of April and into May, the *Gruppe* carried out minelaying missions (a task they had inherited from KG 27) over the Kerch Straits and off Sevastopol on an almost nightly basis. For a brief spell in mid-April they also flew daylight armed reconnaissance sweeps of the Black Sea down as far as the Turkish coast, but with few tangible results.

The ten days of Operation *Trappenjagd* saw I./KG 100 in almost constant action against enemy ground forces that were being forced back on Kerch and thence across the straits to the Kuban. It was while they were thus engaged, on 14 May, that the Soviet destroyer *Dzerzhinski* was lost after hitting a mine laid off Sevastopol during one of the *Gruppe's* earlier missions.

Unlike KG 27, which was moved up to the Kharkov front to participate in *Fridericus* once the Crimea (with the exception of Sevastopol) had been cleared of all Soviet troops, I./KG 100's attentions remained resolutely focused on Black Sea operations. On 15 May it bombed Taman harbour on the far side of the Kerch Straits, causing considerable damage with heavy SC 1800 *Satan* bombs. During the first week of June crews flew up to four missions a day against the defences of Sevastopol, raining every kind of missile down on the beleaguered port from incendiaries to ultra-heavy SC 2500 *Max* bombs. The latter were used in an attempt to demolish the outlying fortifications, including those around Balaklava and the Ölberg.

The tempo of the *Gruppe's* operations increased even more after 7 June – the day that 11. *Armee* launched Operation *Störfang* ('Sturgeon Catch'), the final assault on Sevastopol. I./KG 100 bombed the enemy forts and artillery emplacements guarding the land approaches to the port, as well as the harbour installations and stores and munitions depots. It also sank the 4727-ton transport *Abkhaziya*. On 22 June crews attacked the Soviet submarine base in Inkerman Bay. Five days later aircraft of 2. *Staffel* caught the flotilla leader *Tashkent* evacuating more than 2000 wounded and civilians from Sevastopol. Despite being badly damaged, the 2893-ton destroyer was successfully towed to Novorossisk with 1900 tons of seawater in its riddled hull.

On 28 June Hitler finally launched his long-awaited 1942 summer offensive. I./KG 100 flew its last six missions against Sevastopol on 1 July, the port being captured three days later. By that time the *Gruppe* was already bombing targets in the Caucasus. Its 2 July raid on Novorossisk delivered the *coup de grâce* to the grounded *Tashkent*, sank the 1660-ton destroyer *Bditelny* (which had been instrumental in towing the *Tashkent* in) and damaged the old training cruiser *Komintern*.

One other Heinkel *Gruppe*, II./KG 26, saw service over the Black Sea during the spring of 1942. The torpedo-bombers of 6./KG 26 had been transferred forward from Rumania to Saki, on the Crimea, in January. They were immediately put to work flying armed reconnaissance sweeps against shipping running supplies and reinforcements into Sevastopol, and were also called upon to make nocturnal bombing raids on Sevastopol and the ports along the Caucasian coast.

4. and 5./KG 26 flew in to Saki from Greece in late February, allowing torpedo operations to begin in earnest. They quickly brought results. On the night of 1/2 March one crew severely damaged the 2434-ton steamship *Fabritius*, which had to be beached. Other successes followed, although they were not always as great as the *Gruppe* might have hoped. For example, the three merchant ships claimed on 23 March – one of 5000 tons and the remaining pair of 2000 tons apiece – hardly tally with the loss of a single 2690-ton steamer to aerial torpedo attack admitted by the Soviets on that date. And while an He 111 crew undoubtedly sank the 4125-ton steamship *Svanetiya* with two torpedoes on 17 April, the 28 May attack on an enemy

Russian prisoners-of-war help to load a smaller SC 250 bomb on to a machine of I./KG 100

A He 111 launches the first of two practice torpedoes. In combat it would be suicidal for the machine to remain at this height for long

convoy, escorted by a heavy cruiser and several destroyers, was scathingly dismissed by one senior Luftwaffe officer as 'absolutely pathetic. They fired off 29 torpedoes without any success whatsoever!'

Uniquely, while II./KG 26 was flying torpedo missions over the Black Sea – the southernmost limit of the entire Russian front – another *Gruppe* from the same *Geschwader* was doing the very same thing over the Arctic Ocean, the front's most northerly area of operations. Strictly speaking, of course, the Western Allies' now historic Arctic convoys did not form part of the eastern front proper. But they were an 'integral adjunct' to the war between Germany and the Soviet Union, and the activities of I./KG 26 in opposing them warrant brief coverage here.

Having only recently converted to the torpedo-bomber role, I./KG 26 had moved up from Trondheim-Vaernes to Bardufoss, in northern Norway, in the spring of 1942. Spring was something of a misnomer in this part of the world, however. Bardufoss was situated within a ring of mountains whose peaks rose to heights of 1000 metres and more. When the cloud base was any lower than this, the field could only be approached from a seaward direction along the Malanger Fjord. And at this time of year Bardufoss' single concrete runway was still flanked on either side by five-metre high walls of snow, built up over the course of the winter by constant clearing in order to keep the field operational.

The first convoy that I./KG 26 tried to attack was PQ 13, which had been sighted on 27 March – a week after leaving Iceland bound for Murmansk. The *Gruppe* was briefed for takeoff on 29 March, but only 1. *Staffel* got airborne before the mission was aborted. The weather was closing in fast, with visibility already less than 100 metres in places. 1./KG 26 nonetheless set course for Bear Island, only to be recalled 90 minutes later when radio contact with the reconnaissance aircraft shadowing the convoy was lost. The *Staffel* was lucky to return safely. The weather remained bad the whole time the convoy was within range of Bardufoss, and no further missions were possible.

I./KG 26 had more success just over a month later against convoy PQ 15. More than a dozen of the *Gruppe's* Heinkels lifted off from Bardufoss shortly before midnight on 2 May, and forming up into two waves, they quickly disappeared into the twilight gloom of the Arctic night. The first wave, led by acting *Gruppenkommandeur* Hauptmann Bert Eicke, homed in on the signals from the convoy's 'shadowing' aircraft. The second wave, having to rely on dead reckoning, failed to find the 25 merchantmen of PQ 15, which by this time were midway between the North Cape and Bear Island. Finally, after almost three hours in the air, Hauptmann Eicke sighted one of the destroyers of the convoy's outer screen. An Allied sailor described what happened next;

'Suddenly from the starboard side of the convoy there was a roar of engines and six He 111s came streaking out of the murk almost at water level. From their bellies fell the torpedoes to start on their short run to their targets, while the aircraft zoomed up and over the ships of the convoy. It was a skilful and very bold attack. The pilots paid for their temerity as three bombers crashed into the sea shattered by gunfire, but their skill sent three of their torpedoes speeding straight for ships of the convoy. The Commodore's ship *Botavon* and another, the *Jutland*, shuddered as torpedoes exploded in their sides and they stopped in a sinking condition. But the *Cape Corso*, similarly hit, disintegrated in one tremendous thunderclap as its deadly cargo exploded.'

The entry in the Luftwaffe High Command's war diary for 3 May was remarkably accurate – 'three freighters, totalling 15,808 BRT, sunk'. In fact, these were to be the only merchantmen lost by PQ 15, as the remaining 22 all arrived safely in Murmansk. The Allied claim of three Heinkels shot down is less certain, as the history of KG 26 lists only one crew missing on that date.

Before the month was out the *Gruppe* was in action again, this time against the much larger PQ 16. The convoy came within range of I./KG 26's Heinkels on 27 May, at which point only 11 of the *Gruppe's* machines were serviceable. Crews were briefed to mount a combined attack on PQ 16, together with the dive-bombing Ju 88s of KG 30, but the timing went awry. When the He 111s reached the convoy's position southeast of Bear Island, KG 30 had already carried out its attack and departed. The Heinkels went in singly at low level. This gave each pilot the opportunity to select and line up on a target, but it also meant that every aircraft was subjected in turn to the full weight of the enemy's defensive fire. Two crews were lost. The *Gruppe's* only success was the 5171-ton *Lowther Castle*, which sank after being struck by two torpedoes launched at long range. Two other vessels were claimed as damaged.

I./KG 26 was involved in two further PQ convoy battles, both of which were to take place *after* the start of Hitler's summer offensive in the south. But they are given brief mention here in order to bring the story of the He 111's war in the Arctic to its conclusion.

The 35 merchantmen that made up PQ 17 – the most famous Arctic convoy of all – had sailed from Iceland on 27 June. They did not come under attack from I./KG 26 until the evening of 4 July, however. After taking off from Bardufoss, the *Gruppe's* 26 Heinkels, again led by Hauptmann Eicke, had flown out along Malanger Fjord. Once over open water they adopted *Staffel* line-astern formation and set course for the reported position of the convoy. Before finding it, however, they were themselves sighted by one of the outlying escorts, which promptly raised the alarm.

Now flying line abreast, the *Gruppe* bored in towards the convoy, only to be met by a hail of fire. Most of it was concentrated against the two aircraft that had pulled slightly ahead of the main wave. One of them, commanded by Leutnant Konrad Hennemann, selected the 4841-ton British freighter *Navarino* as its target. The scene was later described by a seaman aboard another of the convoy's vessels;

'The 25 (sic) bombers came roaring in, fast and low, from the starboard quarter. The leading aircraft, ignoring the tempest of fire from all around,

The 'terrible twins' of the early Arctic Convoy battles, namely a Ju 88 dive-bomber of KG 30 (foreground left) and a He 111 torpedo-bomber of KG 26 – to be more precise, 2./KG 26's '1H+GK'

held on till he was well into the convoy before dropping two torpedoes at point-blank range at the *Navarino*. A moment later the bomber crashed in flames just ahead of the escort leader.'

The Heinkel slowly sank beneath the waves, taking Hennemann and his crew with it, as the convoy steamed past on either side. But the two torpedoes had done their work. Damaged beyond repair, the *Navarino* had to be sunk by the escorts – as too did the *William Hooper*, its boiler blown out of the ship by a single torpedo. A third vessel damaged in the attack, the Russian tanker *Azerbaijan*, managed to reach harbour safely. I./KG 26 had thus accounted for just two vessels (for the reported loss of four of its own machines). The vast majority of the 22 merchantmen of PQ 17 that were sunk fell victim to Ju 88 bombers and U-boats after the controversial order for the convoy to 'scatter' was issued later that same evening of 4 July (for more details see *Osprey Combat Aircraft 79 – Junkers Ju 88 Kampfgeschwader on the Russian Front*).

It was more than two months before the next convoy, and the missions flown against PQ 18 were to be the Arctic swansong for the Heinkel torpedo-bombers of I./KG 26. Commanded now by Major Werner Klümper, who until recently had been the chief instructor of the Luftwaffe's principal torpedo school, the *Gruppe* put 24 aircraft into the air late in the afternoon of 13 September. Formating into three waves after exiting Malanger Fjord, the Heinkels headed almost due north, keeping to low level – less than 20 metres above the surface of the water – and maintaining strict radio silence. Behind them followed the bombers of KG 30 and, for the first time, the Ju 88 torpedo-bombers of III./KG 26.

Despite all their precautions, the attackers were picked up by the convoy's long-range radar while still 90 kilometres out. Soon, they rose up above the horizon, looking, in the words of the convoy commodore 'like a huge flight of nightmare locusts'. Keeping in rigid line abreast, the leading Heinkels came in low from the convoy's starboard side, ignoring the wall of shot and shell thrown up in their path. In less than 15 minutes their torpedoes had destroyed eight merchantmen. For the Luftwaffe this was the pinnacle of the entire Arctic convoy campaign.

Although the *Gruppe* despatched another 22 machines to attack PQ 18 on 14 September, they failed to repeat the success of the previous day. Only one ship was sunk (whether by a Heinkel of I./KG 26 or by one of the 18 accompanying Ju 88s of III. *Gruppe* is unclear) and I./KG 26's casualty returns list nine crews missing on this date. Its third and final mission against the convoy, flown on 16 September, consisted of just eight He 111s. The crews scored no successes and suffered no losses. In all, I./KG 26 had lost 12 aircraft in action against PQ 18. Shortly thereafter the *Gruppe* was withdrawn for an urgently needed rest and refit. When it next confronted an Arctic convoy the *Gruppe* too would be flying Ju 88s.

STALINGRAD

itler's long-awaited summer offensive in the south, *Fall Blau* (Case 'Blue'), was finally launched in the early hours of 28 June 1942. With the Soviets still reeling from their recent defeats around Kharkov and in the Crimea, German forces initially made excellent progress. The first phase of the offensive was successfully completed in little more than a week. In order to achieve the twin aims of the operation, the *Führer's* Directive of 23 July then ordered that the forces involved be split into two separate axes of advance, with one to strike due east towards Stalingrad and the other to drive south into the oil-rich Caucasus.

To facilitate this, Army Group South had also been divided into two. Army Group 'A' would head down into the Caucasus, while Army Group 'B' was tasked with taking Stalingrad. And of the two Heinkel *Kampfgeschwader* serving under *Luftflotte* 4 in the south in July 1942, it was Oberst Benno Kosch's KG 55, currently based at Kramatorskaya (*Stab*, II. and III. *Gruppen*) and Kutelnikovo (I. *Gruppe*), west of the Donetz, which would support Army Group 'B's advance on Stalingrad.

This *Geschwader* had already been carrying out individual attacks – both by day and night – against Soviet shipping on the Volga, either side of Stalingrad, for some two weeks or more. Crews had ranged all the way south down to Astrakhan, where the river empties into the Caspian Sea, and as far northwards as Saratov. Then on 17 July, in support of 4. *Panzerarmee's* assault on Rostov, II./KG 55 had given a convincing demonstration of the accuracy of its new Lotfe 7D bombsights (which it

KG 55 demolishes the Don River road bridge at Rostov on 17 July 1942

Machines of KG 55 operating on the southern sector

had acquired two months earlier) by clinically taking out the vital Rostov-Bataisk road bridge across the Lower Don with several direct hits from a height of some 5000 metres. This single strike effectively severed the Soviets' main line of communication – and the Rostov defenders' best route of escape – south into the Caucasus.

In early August II. and III./KG 55 had been transferred down to Samorsk, on the Crimea. The move was ostensibly to give the two *Gruppen* a three-week period of rest and recuperation, but it was not long before their services were being called upon to assist in the fighting in the Caucasus. Samorsk was little more than a 'large field of clover' near the eastern tip of the Crimea. It was not suitable for night operations, but the aircraft of the two *Gruppen* were in the air almost daily, strafing the columns of retreating Soviet troops and bombing the ports along the Caucasian Black Sea coast. It was during one such raid, against Novorossisk on 10 August, that five Heinkels of KG 55 were engaged by a pair of Red Air Force LaGG-3 fighters. The Soviet pilots claimed three of the bombers destroyed, one by a deliberate '*taran*' attack.

While Army Group 'A' continued to drive deep into the Caucasus, units of Army Group 'B' were making rapid progress in their advance on Stalingrad, with 4. *Panzerarmee* following the line of the River Don and General Paulus' 6. *Armee* heading directly across the flat expanse of the great Don Bend. As the main *Kampfgeschwader* supporting the Stalingrad operation, KG 55 was given temporary command of two other Heinkel *Kampfgruppen*, II./KG 27 and I./KG 100.

In the early hours of 16 August the Luftwaffe carried out its first major bombing raid on Stalingrad. The term 'major' is perhaps a little misleading, as the previous weeks and months of constant action had left many *Kampfgruppen* so seriously understrength that they were only able to put as few as nine machines into the air. Nevertheless, this attack marked the start of the remorseless aerial and artillery bombardments that would soon reduce Stalin's namesake city on the Volga to nothing but a mass of ruins. A crewman of I./KG 100 described one of these early daylight raids, flown before the city was totally destroyed;

'A wide band of shimmering silver winds its way through the flat, treeless landscape. Unfettered and untamed, often breaking up into a maze

59

of smaller channels separated by sandbanks and islands, the mass of water that is the Volga flows steadily southwards. Today the visibility is so good that we can just make out the shores of the Caspian Sea, the river's ultimate destination.

'For kilometres along its western bank there are row upon row of wooden huts and houses, looking for all the world like a collection of neatly arranged matchboxes. Nearer the centre a huge grain silo, and a number of large apartment blocks tower above squalid reed-thatched cottages and corrugated-iron shacks. On the river's edge there are oil depots, while factories with long modern assembly halls stretch away to the north.

'Below us, heading across the plain towards the city, are countless tiny black dots, each carefully keeping the same short distance from its neighbour, and each trailing its own plume of dust. These are the tanks and trucks of our ground forces. 6. *Armee* is advancing on Stalingrad!'

On 27 August Oberst Kosch was posted to a training school, and command of KG 55 passed to Oberstleutnant *Dr* Ernst Kühl, hitherto the *Kommandeur* of II. *Gruppe*. By this time the entire *Geschwader* was based at Morozovskaya, little more than 200 kilometres to the southwest of Stalingrad.

As well as keeping up their bombing raids on the city itself, Kühl's *Gruppen* were now flying individual harassing attacks against the complex network of Soviet rear-area railway lines to the east of the Volga. By contrast, there was only one major rail route across the Don Bend from the west into Stalingrad. And as this was being used to capacity by 6. *Armee* as its main supply line, the Luftwaffe's *Kampfgruppen* also found themselves having to undertake their own supply flights to transport bombs and fuel up to their forward bases.

By the end of August the spearheads of 4. *Panzerarmee* had broken through the inner defensive ring to the south of Stalingrad. The opposing sides were still far enough apart for KG 55 to be assigned specific targets within the city. During the first week of September the *Geschwader's* crews were flying anything up to five missions a day, attacking such objectives as the 'Red Barricade' armaments factory, the 'Red October' iron works, the Dzerzhinski tractor factory (which was reported to be turning out tanks) and the Lazur chemical works.

German troops had fought their way to within eight kilometres of the city centre by 3 September, and a week later tanks of 4. *Panzerarmee* reached the banks of the Volga immediately to the south of Stalingrad. Yet despite the constant pounding from ground and air – the Heinkels were now dropping ultra-heavy SC 2500 *Max* bombs on the northern and western districts of the city – the Russians refused to relinquish their hold. They *were* being pushed back towards the river, however, and to disrupt the supplies being ferried across to them from the eastern bank, aircraft of Kühl's *Gruppen* resumed their mining of the waterway by night;

'The Volga glimmers in the pale half-light. We glide towards our assigned stretch of the river and release our two mines unnoticed into the middle of the navigational channel.

'Carefully skirting a known area of flak, we fly south a little closer to Stalingrad. Over the city flares are being fired high into the sky and slowly falling back to earth again. The whole battlefield is bathed in a greenish-white light. Tracers flicker back and forth between the opposing lines.

A He 111 tows a heavily camouflaged Go 242 transport glider low over the Russian countryside

Then, for a few seconds, everything is blackness again. Over there – a ripple of muzzle flashes. An artillery barrage. A moment or two later the bright fiery blossoms of the exploding shells. More flares climb into the night sky. More angry bursts of tracer carve a horizontal web through the darkness. Searchlights spring into life. A stick of bombs from an unseen aircraft somewhere overhead marches in a series of vivid splashes across the ruins. Flak guns begin to bark.'

The tempo of operations was starting to take its toll on the attackers too. I./KG 55 had to be withdrawn and sent down to Saki, in the Crimea, to rest and refit (crews also taking the opportunity to familiarise themselves with their new Lotfe 7D bombsights). The *Gruppe's* place was taken by the glider tugs of III./KG 4, who did not find their time at Stalingrad easy going as they were called upon to undertake both supply flights and bombing missions.

For many of this unit's newer crews, Stalingrad was their baptism of fire in the bombing role. Such was the confusion surrounding their exact duties that the operational orders they received were often contradictory. On at least one occasion they were stopped on the point of taking off for a bombing raid and ordered to change their loads and carry out a supply mission instead. Fortunately, this state of affairs did not last for long. III./KG 4 flew its last bombing sortie over Stalingrad on 27 September, after which it returned to Germany to make ready for an ambitious, but ultimately abortive, glider operation that was intended to capture Astrakhan from the air.

Oberstleutnant *Dr* Kühl lost another of his subordinate *Gruppen* when I./KG 100 also departed Morozovskaya for Saki on 6 October to lend its weight to the fighting in the Caucasus. Exactly a week later, however, the *Gruppe* was back at Stalino to take part in three further bombing raids on Stalingrad, before then being transferred down to Armavir, in the Caucasus. From here it carried out a series of missions, attacking such targets as the Black Sea port of Tuapse and Soviet shipping in the Caspian Sea. Within the month the *Gruppe* had been recalled post-haste to Morozovskaya – the Russians had counter-attacked at Stalingrad and suddenly the German army and its Axis allies were on the defensive!

By the end of October more than 90 per cent of Stalingrad was in German hands. But they were unable to get any further. In the face of fanatical Russian resistance their advance bogged down amidst the ruins of the shattered city. Then, on 19 November, Soviet forces launched a major counter-offensive across the Don to the northwest of Stalingrad, smashing a breach in the line held by the Rumanian 3rd Army and pouring southwards. At the same time a second offensive south of the city struck northwestwards.

Four days later the two claws of this mighty Soviet pincer movement met at Kalach, on the Don, capturing intact the bridge that carried all the supplies by rail into Stalingrad. It had been a perfectly executed *Kessel* or 'cauldron' operation reminiscent of the opening weeks of *Barbarossa*. But this time the troops encircled within the ring of steel were German – nearly a third of a million of them!

The obvious military response to such a situation would be for 6. *Armee* (which formed the vast bulk of the German forces within the Stalingrad perimeter, together with elements of 4. *Panzerarmee* and two Rumanian divisions) to attempt to fight its way out of the trap. But for Hitler, prestige took precedence over military considerations. He was not prepared to countenance any form of retreat – and certainly not one from his arch-enemy's namesake city. Instead, deceived by the earlier success of the Demyansk and Cholm airlift operations, he decreed that the defenders were to stand firm. They would be supplied by air until a relief force could fight its way through to them.

Stalingrad was no Demyansk, however. The amount of food and ammunition required to keep more than 300,000 men adequately supplied was colossal. It was clearly an impossible task. Hitler's obduracy not only sounded the death knell for General Paulus' 6. *Armee*, it also marked the beginning of the end of the war on the eastern front.

The story of the Luftwaffe's desperate attempts to keep Stalingrad supplied from the air really belongs – and quite rightly so – to the 20 or more Ju 52/3m transport *Gruppen* combed from every flying establishment within the Reich and gathered together at Tatsinskaya, just over 250 kilometres west-southwest of Stalingrad. But Oberstleutnant *Dr* Kühl's Heinkel *Kampfgruppen* at Morozovskaya – a good 50 kilometres closer to the beleaguered city – was also to play a significant part in the forthcoming airlift. Firstly, however, its crews were charged with finding out precisely what was happening. VIII. *Fliegerkorps*' order of the day for 19 November reflected the confusion in the German ranks;

'Situation along the northern bend of the Don obscure! All available forces to mount continuous attacks against the points of enemy breakthrough in the north – determine exact positions of leading enemy units!'

But Morozovskaya in the latter half of November was very different to what it had been when KG 55 first took up residence there in late August. There were no hangars on the field. The men lived in earthen bunkers that they had had to dig for themselves. And now cold, rain and snow showers – and temperatures that would soon be hovering between -18 and minus -32 degrees Centigrade – were making that living very hard. The groundcrews, who often had to work through the night, suffered particularly badly. After shovelling the aircraft free from snowdrifts, many got frostbite when they were forced to remove their thick gloves to check the machines' engines and radio equipment with bare hands. Weapons froze and oil solidified. Despite the hard conditions, six crews managed to take off on the morning of 20 November for an armed reconnaissance of the area of the Soviet breakthrough. Two failed to return, including that of Major Hans-Joachim Gabriel, the *Gruppenkommandeur* of II./KG 55.

At 0838 hrs on 24 November VIII. *Fliegerkorps* HQ received an order by radiogram. It was headed '*Führer* Decision' – the highest category of military order in the Wehrmacht – and stated quite baldly, 'present Volga Front and present Northern Front to be held under all circumstances. Air supply'.

Hitler may have made his decision, but it could not alter the basic facts. 6. *Armee* estimated that it needed 500 tons of supplies a day in order to survive and keep on fighting. In turn, Generaloberst von Richthofen, GOC VIII. *Fliegerkorps*, calculated that it would require at least 800 Ju 52/3ms to deliver that amount, and there were only 750 Junkers tri-motor transports in the entire Luftwaffe! However, a '*Führer* Decision' brooked no argument, and moves were immediately put in hand to implement Hitler's demands.

A *'Y-Gerät'*-equipped Heinkel releases its full load of one 500 kg and eight 50 kg bombs over Stalingrad in early September 1942

As a result, Oberstleutnant *Dr* Kühl, *Geschwaderkommodore* of KG 55, found himself shouldering two jobs. As leader of the '*Gefechtsverband* Stalingrad' ('Combat Group Stalingrad') he was responsible for supporting the ground forces in their defence of the River Chir line to the west of the city. This was all that stood between the Red Army and the airfields at Tatsinskaya and Morozovskaya, the Luftwaffe's two main supply bases. And if 'Tatsi' and 'Moro' – as they were commonly known to one and all – were to be captured by the enemy, it would effectively mean the end of the Stalingrad airlift.

In addition, Oberstleutnant *Dr* Kühl was also appointed *Lufttransportführer* 1 and given command of all He 111 units involved in supplying Stalingrad. To augment his seven Heinkel *Kampfgruppen* (five at 'Moro' and two later occupying Millerovo), he was given two He 111-equipped transport *Gruppen* – KGr.z.b.Vs 5 and 20. The former was an established unit, its crews proven veterans of the Demyansk airlift, but the latter was just a motley collection of 54 machines hastily put together from schools and various ancillary units all over the Reich. Some

The second winter of the Russian front soon had the warm-air blowers out again. One of the groundcrew of aircraft 'M' – *Staffel* unknown – prepares to coax its port engine into recalcitrant life

sources state that three further He 111 transport *Staffeln* were flown in from the Mediterranean and added to Kuhl's command at various times during the coming weeks.

At first it seemed as if the weather gods were once again on Hitler's side. On the morning of 25 November, after weeks of atrocious flying conditions, a ridge of high pressure extended eastwards from Poland to the Volga and beyond. By 0300 hrs the ceiling was already at 400 metres. 'Tatsi' and 'Moro' came alive as groundcrews readied their aircraft for the day's operations. By 0900 hrs the clouds had risen to 700 metres and were beginning to break up. Despite this, the Luftwaffe managed to fly only 75 tons of supplies, mostly fuel, into Stalingrad on this first day of the airlift.

Nor did the favourable weather last long. That night high cloud could be seen to the northwest. By the morning of 26 November the cloud base had sunk back down to 200 metres, and frequent snow showers were greatly hampering visibility. The following day a stream of unseasonably warm air brought solid cloud down to just 30 metres in some areas, and loose wet snow reduced visibility to practically zero.

Pictured here earlier in his career as a Hauptmann in front of a He 111 of III./KG 4, Oberstleutnant *Dr* Ernst Kühl – in white cap cover to the right of the propeller blade – was appointed *Lufttransportführer 1* and placed in command of all He 111 units engaged in the Stalingrad airlift

Any machine that did manage to take off and attempt to climb through the dense layer of cloud began icing up at 400 metres – 1000 metres higher and that ice would be two to three centimetres thick. In fact, it was the weather, not the Soviet fighters and flak, that was to prove the airlift's main enemy. On those days – unfortunately all too infrequent – when the winter skies were a crisp clear blue, 'Tatsi' and 'Moro' would be hives of activity with aircraft constantly taking off and landing only minutes apart. Supplies

The Luftwaffe's standard stores container, thousands of which were dropped by parachute over Stalingrad and many of the other eastern front 'fortresses', could either be carried internally in a Heinkel's bomb-bay...

poured in to Stalingrad, although still nowhere near the daily 500 tons demanded by 6. *Armee*. But on other days the 'soup was so thick' that operations had to be scrubbed completely.

On 30 November, just five days after the start of the airlift, VIII. *Fliegerkorps* was relieved of all its combat duties and ordered to concentrate solely on flying supplies in to 6. *Armee*.

The principal airfield within the Stalingrad perimeter was Pitomnik, just over 20 kilometres from the city centre. Of the six landing sites available to the encircled German forces, it alone was adequately equipped to handle large-scale operations, boasting not only lights and a flare path, but also a radio beacon and signals equipment for night operations. A pilot from I./KG 100 describes a supply mission flown in to Pitomnik on 2 December;

'With a full load of provisions and tank shells, we cross the Don and head for Stalingrad. Small patches of cloud give us cover from the enemy's medium flak. Suddenly, four *"Ivans"* (Russian fighters) pop up out of nowhere and stooge about without making any serious attempt to attack us. Whenever one gets a bit too close our gunners give him a short burst. I descend into the clouds, where they can no longer follow us. When we near the landing zone I emerge from the clouds again and we start to search for Pitomnik in the snow-covered landscape below.

'We spot a few aircraft standing about on an open patch of ground. In the gullies surrounding it there are tents and several groups of vehicles. The edge of the field is marked by a red landing cross that is clearly visible against the snow. A green flare rises to meet us – permission to land. I make my approach and put down. A number of machines are parked along one side of the field, Ju 52s and He 111s. Opposite them, on the far side, a couple of fighters obviously being held at readiness.

...or, on later variants of the He 111, attached to the aircraft's ventral weapons rack

This shot of a Heinkel being guided in was purportedly taken at Pitomnik. If so, it must have been during the very early stages of the Stalingrad airlift, for it all seems remarkably peaceful and shows none of the chaos, confusion and wreckage that marked the field's final days

'Everybody lends a hand with the unloading. Our flight engineer syphons precious fuel from the machine – aviation spirit for the fighters from the port wing tank, petrol for the army's Panzers and trucks from the starboard. The wireless-operator unloads the loose supply containers, including several sacks of mail, while the navigator carefully releases the ammunition canisters from the bomb bay. I help wherever I'm needed.

'Empty supply containers are stowed back on board. We are to take four wounded out with us. They clamber laboriously into the aircraft, helped by the wireless-operator. One of them is allowed up into the cockpit behind my seat. We are cleared for takeoff but now, wouldn't you know it, those protective clouds have disappeared and I don't want to get involved with enemy fighters with wounded on board. But it is not long before the pale disc of the sun begins to sink towards the western horizon. It will soon be dark, and the *"Ivans"* will have to start heading home. I take off in the gathering gloom, climb in tight spirals above the field to an altitude of 2000 metres and set course for "Moro".'

By the following day the weather had closed in again, as this wireless-operator/gunner of 5./KG 55 relates;

'We are flying through solid cloud at 2000 metres. The cloud base over Pitomnik is reported to be 300 metres. We head down through the cloud in a steep spiral. The sooner we are out this murk the better, for there are other machines in the vicinity doing exactly the same thing. At 300 metres we do actually break out of the cloud and get our first glimpse of the ground. We can see Pitomnik airfield off to the right ahead of us.

'In the mist surrounding us there are the dim shapes of at least half-a-dozen other machines that, like us, want to get in to Pitomnik. When it's our turn the pilot pulls off a smooth landing, even though the surface of the field is anything but even. We are guided towards a corner where about 20 Heinkels are already standing. Our aircraft is rapidly unloaded and we wait for the wounded that we are to take back with us. In the event, only one is directed over to our machine. The others all have more serious injuries and are stretcher cases, which we cannot accommodate in our Heinkels. Unlike the Junkers, we can only take walking wounded.'

Both the above accounts also describe bombing and strafing attacks made on Pitomnik by Red Air Force fighters and *Shturmoviks* while the Heinkels were on the ground waiting to take off. The enemy fighters and the 'Flak alleys' lining the Heinkels' known approach routes into the Stalingrad pocket were indeed making things difficult for the crews flying the airlift. But the weather remained the major foe. Heavy fog prevented operations on the morning of 5 December, although some 17 He 111s were able to get off later in the day. Together with about 50 Ju 52/3ms, they managed to deliver close on 150 tons of supplies to Stalingrad's defenders – a creditable performance, but still woefully short of what was needed.

At Morozovskaya, KG 55's met officer was being driven nearly to despair. On 6 December he wrote;

'Day after day nothing but bad weather with fog, low-lying clouds and often snowstorms either here or in the fortress [i.e. Stalingrad] so that our machines are unable to fly, or perhaps just once a day at best – and that only under the most difficult of conditions. Sometimes the weather in the fortress is clear, but it's bad here. Then those at the other end can't understand why no aircraft are arriving. They begin to have their doubts about us, and complain loudly.'

It was on 6 December that the commander of a Millerovo-based Heinkel of II./KG 27 flew in to Pitomnik on a mission of a different kind;

'We landed at Pitomnik late on the 6th with orders to fly out a general early the following morning. We spent the night in an underground bunker close to the field. During the night an infantry hauptmann came by and wanted to commandeer my crew to fight in his assault squad. Our passenger prevented this. He turned out to be Generalmajor Friedrich Schulz, Chief-of-Staff of the newly established *Heeresgruppe* (Army Group) Don, who had gone into Stalingrad to assess the situation for himself.'

And that situation was growing ever more critical. On 12 December an armoured corps of 4. *Panzerarmee* launched an attempt to relieve Stalingrad from the southwest. It fought its way to within 48 kilometres of the perimeter before being forced to a halt on 21 December. The following day the Germans' worst fears were realised. Reports started to come in that the Russians had broken through the River Chir line and were advancing on Tatsinskaya. In the early hours of 24 December Soviet tanks burst onto the overcrowded field and started firing into the mass of aircraft. Incredibly – despite visibility of little more than 500 metres and a ceiling of only 30 metres – 124 Ju 52/3ms (some flown by their crew-chiefs) managed

This was one unknown crew's humorous take on their airlift duties. A bedraggled airman, who appears to be sweating blood and is wearing an armband indicating KG 55, pushes a wheelbarrow loaded with boxes marked 'Cigarettes' and 'Cognac'. In reality they would more likely be transporting ammunition and loaves of dry bread

to scramble into the air amidst all the confusion. But the total loss of 46 others, plus the abandonment of much valuable equipment and the capture by the enemy of hundreds of tons of supplies destined for 6. *Armee* was an enormous blow.

Morozovskaya was also under serious threat, but the Soviets were repulsed by local ground forces who were ably assisted by units of the Luftwaffe, including the He 111s of KG 55;

'We are quickly reloaded with bombs – one 500 kg and ten 50 kg. Heavy snow. The *Kette* sticks close together. Nothing to be seen of the enemy within a radius of 10-20 kilometres of the field. We turn back. Weather simply too bad. As we are banking I spot through the mist the faint glow of a fire to the north of us. We fly towards it, only to be met with heavy flak. A few cottages. Alongside them a truck and four, five or six tanks. One of the cottages is burning – that was the glow I had seen. I can make out the Soviet stars on the tanks. They have probably stopped to refuel. Hurriedly arm the bombs – are the fuzes delayed-action or not – can't remember. Never mind, just let them go! They fall into the middle of the group of tanks. "Direct hit!" the gunner yells.

'As we curve away I can see fires and explosions behind us. But we've caught a packet too, either from our own bombs – height of release was only about 20 metres – or from the enemy's flak. The starboard engine has given up the ghost and the cockpit is full of smoke. Slowly we crab our way southeast across the snow-covered steppe back towards "Moro".'

The Soviet threat had been averted for the moment, but the Heinkels' days at Morozovskaya were clearly numbered. Nevertheless, the machines of I./KG 100, which had been evacuated to Novocherkassk on 24 December as a precautionary measure, were back the following day. And on 30 December KG 55 welcomed the return of III. *Gruppe* from

There was very little to laugh about in reality. Here, a winter-camouflaged He 111 burns out on the flat featureless steppe. Fortunately, the pilot was able to put it down on German-held territory and the crew escaped captivity – or worse its two-month sojourn on the Crimea. As the year drew to a close the weather deteriorated even further. Violent snowstorms resulted in metre-high snowdrifts. Plummeting temperatures made it ever harder to coax the machines' engines into life. Icing became a major problem. In the space of just eight days the airlift lost 62 aircraft to this one cause alone!

On 2 January 1943, a day when 'Moro' was again shrouded in thick fog, the now Oberst *Dr* Kühl decided it was finally time to evacuate his *Gruppen* to Novocherkassk. Lanterns were placed at intervals along the runway and most of the fully loaded aircraft got off the ground without undue difficulty. Unlike the Ju 52/3ms' mad scramble to escape from Tatsinskaya, the He 111s were able to take a lot of equipment with them when they left. Oberst *Dr* Kühl and a small staff remained behind at Morozovskaya in the hope that the evacuation might only be temporary. But it was not to be, as 48 hours later Soviet tank shells began exploding on the field. 'Moro' – and with it one of the largest stores depots of 6. *Armee* – had to be blown up. Oberst *Dr* Kühl joined his *Gruppen* at Novocherkassk, which was almost twice as far away from Stalingrad as Morozovskaya, to continue airlift operations from there as best he could.

Meanwhile, conditions at Pitomnik were also growing steadily worse;

'The flat landscape west of Stalingrad was just one single, monotonous blanket of snow. But Pitomnik was easy enough to find, surrounded as it was by an unbroken ring of hundreds of wrecked aircraft that had either come to grief on landing or takeoff, or had been destroyed on the ground by air attack or artillery fire, and which had been unceremoniously pushed aside to keep the vital runway clear.

'Every time we landed there we wondered whether our own machine would end up being added to the pile of wreckage. But the look of utter despair on the faces of the emaciated troops who came shuffling forward to help us unload, the dull flicker of hope in the eyes of the wounded wondering whether we would take them out with us, soon drove such thoughts from our minds.

'While the others concentrated on emptying the aircraft of its supplies and excess fuel, I went to fetch some of the wounded. When I poked my head into one of the large Red Cross tents the stench was appalling! Hundreds of wounded lay packed together on the bare earth that had once been covered by a thin layer of straw, but was now nothing but a matted carpet of dirt and filth. I quickly found seven wounded who assured me that they were in a fit state to walk the 200 metres out to the machine. But after the first few metres they sank to the ground and I had to drag them the rest of the way. They squirmed in agony and cursed me roundly for not stopping, even for a moment. But I had to hurry, as there were always enemy fighter-bombers lurking nearby waiting to pounce on any aircraft that stayed too long on the ground.'

They may not have appreciated the fact at the time, but those seven unknown wounded were among the lucky ones. On 10 January the Soviets launched a massive assault on the Stalingrad perimeter. Six days later the Red Army overran Pitomnik airfield. The recent loss of 'Tatsi' and 'Moro' had been major, but not fatal, setbacks to airlift operations. Aircraft were still flying in from further afield (some from as far away as Taganrog on the Sea of Azov). But the capture of Pitomnik was a disaster from which Stalingrad could not possibly recover.

From now on most supplies would have to be air-dropped. This may have been of some slight benefit to the weary Heinkel crews, for it meant the end of the increasingly dangerous landings and takeoffs within the perimeter that had resulted in so many crashes. Their machines would now also be spared the agonising turnaround on the ground at Pitomnik, where they routinely came under enemy fire. Finally, mission lengths were reduced too.

But for the defenders of Stalingrad the consequences of losing Pitomnik were stark. The amount of supplies flown in to them decreased sharply to well below 100 tons per day. As the perimeter shrank, many containers fell beyond their reach or into the hands of the Russians. And, of course, their wounded could no longer be flown out.

Inside the perimeter desperate steps were taken to try to rectify the situation. Gumrak, Stalingrad's second airfield, was considered a lost cause. Three machines of III./KG 55 had tried to land there late on 18 January, and although one had succeeded in doing so, it was never heard from again. Another made ten attempts to get down but finally had to abandon the effort, the provisional runway being far too short and partly blocked by scattered wreckage. In the end the crew had to airdrop the 20 sacks of bread they were carrying. The third aircraft did the same.

Now the field was completely blocked by wrecked aircraft and already under threat from Soviet forces. References give the date of its ultimate capture by the Russians as either 21 or 23 January. Bassargino, once a forward landing ground of the Red Air Force but now hardly more than a tiny strip of churned-up meadow, was in a similar condition. And both Karpovka and Gorodichi were too close to the fighting and coming under heavy artillery and infantry fire.

The last hope was Stalingradskiy, a small field much bombed and only some three kilometres from the city centre. 6. *Armee* engineers did what they could to effect repairs, reporting it operational and ready to receive aircraft on the afternoon of 22 January. However, when the first He 111s tried to land there, six (including three from KG 55) crashed as a result of the bomb craters hidden beneath the thick snow. Several dozen others managed to get down before darkness fell. They would be among the last aircraft to touch down within the perimeter. It had been decided that it would be too dangerous to attempt night landings at Stalingradskiy. And the very next day the Soviets launched a heavy assault on the western outskirts of Stalingrad, splitting the Germans inside the ruined city into two separate pockets and capturing the airfield at Stalingradskiy in the process.

Now the defenders were entirely reliant on airdrops, but the end was approaching rapidly. On 28 January the southern pocket was itself split in two. Forty-eight hours later Soviet forces reached Red Square, the very heart of Stalingrad. The following day, 31 January, the newly promoted Generalfeldmarschall Paulus, GOC 6. *Armee*, surrendered to the Russians, along with 14 of his generals. That same night 110 transport aircraft headed for the northern pocket, where fighting was still going on. The troops on the ground had laid out an illuminated, triangular-shaped drop zone among the rubble. It was marked with a swastika of red lamps. This enabled nearly 100 of the machines to find and release their loads on target. The next night about 85 of the 108 aircraft despatched managed to do the same.

Few forward landing grounds had any proper facilities. At night a row of lanterns might indicate the runway. By day a few bits of evergreen dumped in the snow served the same purpose

The drop zone was still visible during the evening hours of 2 February, but then disappeared at around midnight. The first 12 He 111s of that night's airdrop had been instructed to report the situation over the drop zone by radioing back one of three prearranged codewords. Of the 11 that reached the pocket, seven crews reported that they had seen nothing and had made no drops. Three dropped part of their loads, and the last thought they had detected signs of activity. On the strength of this latter signal, the remaining 16 Heinkels were despatched. At debriefing upon their return, the crews reported what they had seen. They stated that the outline of the northern pocket was no longer clearly identifiable. Lights were burning throughout the whole area and a large fire was raging in the northwestern corner of the Dzerzhinski tractor works. A convoy of vehicles with its lights full on was approaching the works from the northeast. Parachute flares illuminated the ruins, but there were no signs of continued fighting.

The Battle of Stalingrad was over. It is not known which Heinkel units took part in those final missions over the city in the early hours of 3 February. One likely contender is the *Stabskette* (HQ Flight) of KG 26, which had been sent to southern Russia at the end of 1942 and there incorporated into KGr.z.b.V.23 – one of the last Heinkel transport *Gruppen* to be cobbled together specifically for Stalingrad airlift duties – in January 1943. KG 26's unit history states quite categorically that 'the last three supply aircraft to fly over the already-fallen Stalingrad were those of the erstwhile *Stabskette*'.

What *is* known is that Oberst *Dr* Kühl's KG 55 and its subordinate *Gruppen* had continued to airdrop supplies into Stalingrad until the very end. Between 29 November 1942 and 2 February 1943 the Heinkels of KG 55 carried out no fewer than 2566 supply flights into the besieged city (an average of some 40 missions a day, but in reality a much higher figure than that when the many days of bad weather that prevented flying are taken into account). Those flights resulted in the delivery of very nearly 3300 tons of supplies, including some 1540 tons of foodstuffs, 1110 tons of fuel and nearly 700 tons of ammunition.

The Stalingrad airlift cost the Luftwaffe 488 transport aircraft lost, missing or damaged beyond repair – 165 of that total had been Heinkel He 111s.

THE LONG ROAD TO DEFEAT

The Battle of Stalingrad ended in the annihilation of 20 German divisions and the capture of something like a quarter-of-a-million men. It was a disaster of such cataclysmic proportions that events taking place on other sectors of the eastern front were totally overshadowed while the drama on the Volga was being played out.

Yet the actions fought by those units – including the Heinkel *Kampfgeschwader* – not involved over Stalingrad were very real, and often very bitter none the less. The neat Orders of Battle that had been in place at the start of *Barbarossa*, with each *Geschwader* being responsible for operations solely within 'its' particular sector, were long a thing of the past. As a result of the many Russian counter-attacks since the end of 1941, the Luftwaffe's combat *Geschwader*, *Gruppen* and even individual *Staffeln* were now being shuttled back and forth ever more frequently to wherever each new danger threatened. Despite the 'fire brigade' nature of many of the Heinkels' operations from mid-1942 onwards, the clearest overview of their activities can still best be gained by considering each sector in turn.

The most static of the three main sectors of the Russian front was undoubtedly that in the north. After Vlasov's abortive counter-offensive across the River Volkhov and the relief of the twin pockets of Demyansk and Cholm, the northern front had returned to some semblance of stability. German forces continued to besiege Leningrad while managing to hold off Soviet thrusts elsewhere in the sector. The only Heinkel *Kampfgruppe* in the north during the summer of 1942 had been Major Fritz Pockrandt's I./KG 53. From its base west of Schlüsselburg, the unit's operations during that time had consisted of the usual mix of bombing raids on Leningrad, army support missions, sweeps over the Baltic Sea and longer range strikes on the Soviets' rear-area supply networks.

In September I. *Gruppe* was joined in the north by II. and III./KG 53, both up from brief spells of duty on the central sector. And it was on the boundary between the northern and central sectors that the Red Army was now setting its sights again as it prepared for yet another offensive – one that would result in a 'mini-Stalingrad' that is all but forgotten today.

The terrain between Army Groups North and Centre was one of forests, lakes and swamps. In the middle of it, forming a kind of island base for the Germans, was the town of Velikiye Luki, an important road and rail junction described by one contemporary historian as 'the strongest hedgehog defence base on the central front'. The Soviet assault, launched on 25 November, closed the ring around Velikiye Luki in just two days, trapping 7000 German troops within the town. The commander on the

For much of the latter half of 1942, while the battle for Stalingrad was unfolding far to the south, the only Heinkels on the northern sector were those of KG 53. Here, flanked by an impressive array of ordnance, a machine of I. *Gruppe* sits on a corrugated dispersal point constructed of felled logs to prevent it from sinking into the autumn mud

ground urged that the garrison should be allowed to break out immediately. Predictably, Hitler flatly refused, declaring that the defenders would have to hold on until contact could be restored.

As at Stalingrad, the *Kommodore* of a Heinkel *Kampfgeschwader* was placed in command of air support and supply operations. In this instance it was Oberst Karl-Eduard Wilke of KG 53, who was named *Gefechtsverbandsführer Welikije Luki* (Battle-Group Leader Velikiye Luki). Among the various units – including Stukas and fighters – that made up Wilke's command would be four *Gruppen* of He 111 bombers, namely his own I. and III./KG 53, reinforced later by the central sector's II. and III./KG 4.

Although admittedly on a far smaller scale, the events that followed were remarkably similar to what took place at Stalingrad. A relief force tried to fight its way through to the town but was brought to a halt just short of establishing contact. And, before finally succumbing, the 'fortress' of Velikiye Luki (the *Führer's* description) was split into two separate pockets.

As at Stalingrad, the weather played a significant role. The worsening conditions allowed support and supply operations to be flown on only 37 of the defenders' 55-day fight for survival. The small area actually occupied by the encircled troops also brought difficulties of its own for the crews of the Heinkels, especially after the garrison was divided into two at the end of the year, with the main body around the railway station in the eastern suburbs and a much smaller force holding out in the old Kremlin, or citadel, on the western edge of the town;

'The problem of dropping supplies by parachute in horizontal flight into such a confined area as the citadel, which measured only some 250 x 100 metres, proved insoluble. We tried everything – using the low cloud ceiling, "lobbing" the containers in by climbing just prior to the point of release, dropping by dusk and at night – but nothing really worked. Only the Stukas, equipped with supply containers for the first time at Velikiye Luki, were able to dive on the target with pinpoint accuracy.

'As soon as the Russians realised that we were relying to a great extent on signal fires to guide us in on our final approach, they started lighting more and more fires around the citadel and eastern station. This made accurate dropping almost impossible.'

In early December the Heinkels of I. and III./KG 53 were joined by those of III./KG 4. The latter unit was the glider-tug *Gruppe* that had flown its last bombing mission over Stalingrad on 27 September and then been pulled out of the line to prepare for the projected air assault on Astrakhan. When this operation failed to materialise, III./KG 4 had been despatched to southern Italy, where it reverted to its intended role by towing Go 242 gliders loaded with fuel across the Mediterranean to Rommel's forces in North Africa. On 3 December the *Gruppe* had been hurriedly ordered back to the eastern front. It landed at Smolensk-North, 'where the thermometer was showing 20 degrees below zero – something of a shock for those crews still wearing tropical kit!'

Although III./KG 4's first mission was a bombing attack on enemy troops on 10 December, crews soon found themselves engaged in supply flights as well, towing gliders of *Verbindungskommando* (S) V (Communications Detachment (Glider) V) into Velikiye Luki at low level both by day and by night. These were extremely difficult and hazardous undertakings, and heavy losses were inevitable. The glider pilots had to put their Gothas down in the most confined spaces – towards the end of the siege, within the walls of the citadel itself. For them such missions were true *Himmelfahrtskommandos* (literally 'Ascension Day Detachments', or 'One-way tickets to Heaven'), for once inside Velikiye Luki they stood very little chance of getting out again.

On 25 December II./KG 4 became the fourth and final He 111 *Gruppe* to be assigned to Wilke's *Gefechtsverband Welikije Luki*, but the town and its defenders could not be saved. A second relief attempt was launched on 4 January 1943. Ten days later this column was also halted just a few hundred metres short of the citadel. Finally, on 15 January, the garrison received permission to break out. Of the 7000 men who had been surrounded in the town less than two months earlier, only 176 – all from the citadel pocket in the west – managed to do so.

The battle for Velikiye Luki had thus involved four of the six Heinkel *Kampfgruppen* operating on the northern and central sectors. But what of the other two? I./KG 4 had seen heavy fighting around the Vyazma and Tula areas before being withdrawn from the central sector in December 1942. Handing its surviving aircraft over to II./KG 4, this *Gruppe* was then transferred back to Germany by rail, firstly to enjoy a short spell of leave, which was to be followed by many months spent re-equipping and retraining on the four-engined Heinkel He 177.

II./KG 53 had likewise returned to Germany in December 1942 after being in continuous action on the northern sector throughout the autumn. Its period of rest and recuperation in the homeland was to be short-lived, however. In the second week of January the *Gruppe* was ordered to leave Greifswald for Voroshilovgrad, on the River Donetz. From here crews were to participate in the dying days of the Stalingrad airlift. But with Pitomnik on the point of capture and Gumrak soon to follow, there was very little the Heinkels of II./KG 53 could do;

'Marker flares had been laid out in a large open square somewhere near the middle of the northern pocket. This is where we were to drop our supply containers by parachute from an altitude of 200 metres. But after doing so we still had ten sacks of loaves and other foodstuffs on board. These had to be pushed out separately through the ventral hatch, which meant making several passes over the area at a height of only some 30-50 metres.

'The scene beneath our wings was like looking into the gates of Hell. A flickering sea of lights, fires and explosions. The flashes of artillery fire, the glaring fingers of searchlights clawing the night sky trying to catch us, the dense barrage of light flak through which we had to fly every time we came in to make another drop. As we roared low across the dropping zone flares would be shot

Diverted temporarily from the final stages of the Stalingrad airlift, this aircraft of KG 27 makes use of a brief window of fine weather in January 1943 to deliver its lethal load 'somewhere on the Don front'. The Kopfring (literally 'head ring') around the nose of the SC 1000 Hermann bomb was to stop it penetrating too deeply into the ground before exploding, thus maximising its blast effect

up at us, bathing the whole area of the square in an unearthly green light. We could make out every detail on the ground below, even individual soldiers flitting like ghostly apparitions between the ruins.'

Delivering the loaves of bread cost the *Gruppe* dear. By the time Stalingrad fell, and after little more than two weeks in action, II./KG 53 had been reduced to just ten crews.

Meanwhile, far to the south, the latter half of 1942 had seen Army Group 'A' advance deep into the Caucasus. Its progress was spectacular. The important centres of Maikop, Krasnodar and Mozdok had all been taken before the end of August. In September German forces captured the Black Sea port of Novorossisk on the west coast of the Caucasus and were closing in on Astrakhan to the east. By the end of October they were threatening the Grozny oilfields, but there the offensive stalled. Adopting a rigorous 'scorched earth' policy, the Russians had already fired the oil wells at Maikop and the refineries at Krasnodar before withdrawing. The glittering prize of Caucasia's oil had eluded Hitler.

Then, in December 1942, the Soviets counter-attacked. Army Group 'A's' retreat from the Caucasus during the winter of 1942/43 was to be even more precipitate than its autumn advance southwards. And, in the end, all the Wehrmacht had to show for its six months of hard campaigning were some impressive propaganda shots of German mountain troops hoisting the swastika flag atop Mount Elbrus, the tallest peak in the Caucasus and Europe's highest mountain.

Army Group 'A's' units had not had a regular He 111 presence supporting them throughout the whole of their Caucasian venture, but a number of Heinkel *Kampfgruppen* – among them III./KG 4, II./KG 26, II./KG 27 and I./KG 100 – *did* operate over the area at specific times and against specific targets. The latter included the remains of the Soviet Black Sea Fleet, now holed up in Poti harbour close to the border with Turkey, and the Astrakhan supply road, part of the overland route used to carry Allied aid up to the Soviet Union from Persia (Iran).

By the spring of 1943 Hitler's armies were on the defensive everywhere. The Red Army had driven a narrow corridor through to Leningrad in the north (although the city would not be completely liberated until January 1944) and

By the late spring of 1943 the Heinkel *Kampfgruppen* **on the Russian front had again shed their winter coats, as witness this anonymous I.** *Gruppe* **machine going about its business over the central sector**

was pushing hard all along the central sector, threatening to cut off those Germans still attempting to escape from the Caucasus in the south. The *Führer's* quandary now was how to regain the initiative. The grandiose aims of his last two eastern front summer offensives – *Barbarossa* in 1941 aimed at nothing less than bringing the Soviet Union to its knees, while *Blau/Braunschweig* in 1942 intended to capture Stalingrad and gain access to the oilfields of the Caucasus – had both ended in total failure.

In 1943 he was forced to set his sights a little lower. Russian pressure on the central sector had driven a huge bulge – some 120 kilometres deep and almost 180 kilometres wide from north to south – into the German lines around the town of Kursk. Operation *Zitadelle* was designed to 'pinch off' this bulge by launching simultaneous attacks on its northern and southern edges and then destroy the Soviet forces trapped inside it. The Luftwaffe gathered close on 2000 combat aircraft in preparation for the forthcoming operation. This represented nearly three-quarters of its entire available strength on the Russian front and included all ten Heinkel *Kampfgruppen* currently operational in the east.

Under the newly established *Luftflotte* 6 to the north of the bulge were II. and III./KG 4 which, together with I. and III./KG 53, were based on fields around Karachev and Bryansk (I./KG 4 and II./KG 53 were both in Germany refitting and re-equipping). South of the bulge, as part of *Luftflotte* 4, were ranged all three *Gruppen* of KG 27, plus the eight machines of that *Geschwader's* specialised train-busting *Staffel*, 14.(*Eis.*)/KG 27. First entering service in February 1943, the '*Eis.*' in this unit's designation was an abbreviation of *Eisenbahn*, meaning 'railway'. KG 27 was concentrated at Dnepropetrovsk and Zaporozhe. Also under *Luftflotte* 4 but closer to the front, at Kharkov-East and Stalino, were II. and III./KG 55. The original I./KG 55 had been returned to Germany some two months earlier and there re-designated to become III./LG 1. A new I./KG 55 had then been formed from KGr.z.b.V. 5, the veteran He 111 transport *Gruppe* of the Stalingrad airlift, but this was still undergoing retraining at Wiesbaden.

Finally, on 4 July – the very eve of *Zitadelle* – the He 111s of I./KG 100, having only recently returned from three weeks training on the Lotfe 7D bombsight in the south of France, had moved up from Stalino to Poltava, thereby bringing *Luftflotte* 4's total number of Heinkel *Kampfgruppen* to six.

One of the ten Heinkel *Kampfgruppen* taking part in *Zitadelle* was III./KG 55. This photograph, taken in the summer of 1943, shows Hauptmann Oskar Dettke (the *Kapitän* of 9. *Staffel*) upon the completion of his 300th combat mission. Note the *Staffel's* 'Snorting bull' emblem above the celebratory garland on the machine's tail

Despite the indifferent quality of this photograph, the unique positioning of the yellow theatre bands on these Heinkels unmistakably identify them as aircraft of I./KG 100 – another *Gruppe* that participated in the Battle of Kursk

Just as the Luftwaffe's major players at Stalingrad had been the Ju 52/3m transport *Gruppen*, so the aerial brunt of the *Zitadelle* offensive was undoubtedly borne by the Stuka and ground-attack units of *Luftflotten* 4 and 6. Once again, however, the Heinkel *Kampfgruppen* were to make a significant, if little known, contribution to this latest operation by attacking enemy troop and tank concentrations in the field, and by bombing the Soviets' rear-area lines of communication and supply.

Zitadelle was launched in the early hours of 5 July 1943, and the He 111s were involved from the very outset. On the northern shoulder the first machines of II./KG 4 began taking off from Sechinskaya at 0325 hrs to bomb enemy positions in the path of 9. *Armee's* push southwards. During the course of the next week, together with *Luftflotte* 6's three other Heinkel *Kampfgruppen*, they would carry out three or four such missions a day, constantly pounding the Soviet defences in direct support of their own ground forces.

Along the southern edge of the Kursk bulge the Heinkels of *Luftflotte* 4 were no less active in their support of 4. *Panzerarmee's* advance northwards. In just eight days the crews of KG 55's two *Gruppen* notched up a total of 899 individual sorties. Some 178 of these were flown on 7 July alone, when the He 111 crews were instructed to place their bombs no more than 200 metres in front of the leading Tiger tanks of II. SS-*Panzerkorps*!

Meanwhile, in support of *Armee-Abteilung* (Army Detachment) Kempf, I./KG 100 was engaging the enemy's infantry – a task its crews did not altogether relish;

'The orders at briefing were clear – "Attack enemy troop concentrations". It sounded straightforward enough, but what did it really mean?

'It meant loading our machines with three AB 500 weapons canisters, each of which contained 392 SD 1 anti-personnel bomblets weighing just one kilogram apiece. After release, the canisters were blown apart some 1000 metres above the ground, strewing their deadly contents over a wide area. If a formation of 30 aircraft dropped their loads over an area measuring 900 x 100 metres, it was the equivalent of an explosion in every square metre! From our release height of 4000 metres all we could see was a harmless little flicker of sparks spreading across the ground below. To any infantry unit unlucky enough to be caught in such a bombardment, it was like having 35,000 hand-grenades hurled at it all at once!

'Another weapon we employed against enemy columns was the ten-kilogram SD 10 fragmentation bomb. Our machines could carry 128 of these little beasts. Because of its highly sensitive fuse, the SD 10 did not dig itself into the earth but detonated on the surface, sending hundreds of tiny 13-gram fragments

of metal flying almost horizontally over a radius of some 25 metres.

'Both these weapons were highly unpopular with the crews. The one-kilogram bombs were packed live in to their containers. The SD 10s were also armed prior to the mission. Any takeoff accident or flak hit *en route* to the target could quite easily set the whole bomb load off, which inevitably meant the end of the aircraft and of the crew flying it.'

At the other end of the scale, in the month prior to *Zitadelle* most of the eastern front's He 111 *Kampfgruppen* had joined forces to fly a brief series of purely strategic nocturnal bombing missions. Their primary target had been the tank factory at Gorki, nearly 400 kilometres to the northeast of Moscow – more precisely, that plant's 'Molotov Combine' works, which alone covered an area of four square kilometres, and was reportedly turning out 800 T-34 tanks a week.

At 2000 hrs on the evening of 4 June the first of 128 Luftwaffe bombers (He 111s and Ju 88s) took off for the six-hour round trip to Gorki. They were loaded with a wide variety of bombs, ranging from 1700-2500 kg 'aerial mines' to 70 kg HE and 50 kg fragmentation bombs, as well as heavy oil bombs and thousands of incendiaries. These loads were to be dropped in specific sequences to ensure that the maximum amount of damage would be caused, and every crew had been instructed to keep to a strict timetable.

On that first night of 4/5 June 1943, the raiders dropped 179 tons of bombs in all. But a target the size of the 'Molotov Combine' could not be knocked out in one strike. The following night 154 aircraft delivered 242 tons of bombs. They returned again the next night, and the next, after which the *Kampfgruppen* carried out two attacks on the industrial rubber plants at Yaroslavl, north of Moscow, and one on the oil refineries at Saratov far to the southeast, before staging three final raids on Gorki on 10, 13 and 22 June.

Reconnaissance photos revealed extensive damage to the 'Molotov Combine' works. It was estimated that 800 tanks – a full week's output – had been destroyed in the raids, and that production was halted completely for the next six weeks. Despite the flak and nightfighters defending the plants, relatively few bombers had been lost. II./KG 4, for example, reported two aircraft failing to return from a total of 122 individual sorties flown.

This short series of strategic night raids had been judged a great success. More importantly for the crews involved, perhaps, was the feeling that they had at last been employed in their

It was shortly after *Zitadelle* that II./KG 53 returned to the central sector of the eastern front after a period of rest and re-equipment in the Reich. Initially based at Olsufyevo, near Bryansk, 'A1+AC' of the *Gruppenstab* displays its still immaculate finish

An impressive close-up of the 'front office' of a Heinkel, whose cheerful crew seem to be more interested in the photographer than in watching where they are going!

There can have been few smiles on the faces of the crew aboard 5./KG 4's 'KN' as they struggled back to Orel-West after suffering a *'taran'* attack during their 7/8 June night raid on the 'Molotov Combine' tank factory at Gorki

Later on that same 8 June 1943, a reconnaissance machine of 1.(F)/100 took this photo of the 'Molotov Combine' showing the cumulative effects of the previous four nights' raids

proper role following months almost exclusively spent on defensive ground-support missions in the aftermath of Stalingrad. And yet, as already described in this chapter, less than a fortnight later at Kursk they were once again being used – maybe 'misused' would be the more accurate – in direct support of ground operations.

Nevertheless, the strategic bombing lesson appeared to have been learnt, even if a little tardily. On 26 November 1943, after the Heinkel *Kampfgruppen* had spent another three months occupied primarily in the support of the ground forces, who were now being steadily pushed back on all sectors, Luftwaffe C-in-C Hermann Göring issued the following statement;

'In order to undertake a systematic air offensive against Russia's armaments industry, I intend to gather together the bulk of the bomber units serving in the east, reinforced by special pathfinder units, under the command of the GOC IV. *Fliegerkorps*. The task of these units will be to carry out annihilating attacks against Russian industrial targets in order to prevent the mass of tanks, guns and aircraft being produced from reaching the front, thereby denying them to the enemy and, at the same time, bringing greater relief to our own hard-pressed eastern army than would otherwise be achieved by battlefield support operations alone.'

It was a noble sentiment, and one, moreover, that made good military sense. But, as many critics of the *Reichsmarschall* pointed out, it came far too late in the day. The proper time for such action had been two years earlier, in the autumn of 1941, when the Soviet Union was still reeling from the blow of *Barbarossa*. Now, despite the evidence of Gorki, the growing might of the Red Air Force and the Luftwaffe's own declining fortunes would make any operations of this kind difficult to mount and hazardous to execute.

A month before Göring's announcement there had been a minor organisational change in the Heinkel units' order of battle. On 21 October I./KG 100 had transferred from Nikolayev to Kirovograd, where it was immediately re-designated to become the new I./KG 4. At the same time the original I./KG 4, still in the throes of its conversion to the He 177 at

Lechfeld, in southern Germany, adopted the mantle of I./KG 100. The Luftwaffe's Heinkel presence in the east thus now comprised exactly the same four *Kampfgeschwader* as at the start of the campaign, namely KGs 4, 27, 53 and 55.

However, with KGs 27 and 53 (and the new I./KG 4) at present fully committed on the southern sector covering the ground forces' fighting retreat across the Ukraine and withdrawal from the Crimea, Göring's ambitious plans to 'gather together the bulk of the bomber units serving in the east' to create a strategic strike force had initially

The original of this unusual shot of a Heinkel bomber is captioned as being taken on the eastern front by a war photographer flying in the machine almost immediately above it. The image was dated 7 December 1943, but if this was indeed the case, where was the snow?

to be scaled down to just seven *Kampfgruppen* (including two equipped with Ju 88s) totalling little more than 150 machines in all.

Within days of the *Reichsmarschall's* decree, the five Heinkel *Gruppen* serving under IV. *Fliegerkorps* on the central sector had been withdrawn from operations and pulled back to airfields in Poland to embark upon a lengthy period of training for their new role as a dedicated strategic bomber force. II. and III./KG 4 both retired the 350 kilometres from Puchovichi, southeast of Minsk, to Bialystok, where the crews were quartered in a local tank barracks. KG 55, scattered further afield, was gathered together on two neighbouring bases to the south of Warsaw – Deblin-Irena (*Stab*, II. and III. *Gruppen*) and Deblin-Ulez (I. *Gruppe*). The former was an established airfield, whilst the latter was 'just a bare patch of grass lacking any facilities whatsoever'.

While training in Poland the Heinkels came under the *'Auffrischungsstab Ost'* (literally, the 'Refurbishment Staff East'), which was a cover name temporarily adopted by the otherwise currently redundant IV. *Fliegerkorps* to deceive the enemy. Despite the harsh winter conditions the training itself was extensive and thorough. The *Gruppen* received new aircraft (the latest model He 111H-16s and H-20s) and were slowly brought back up to full establishment. The crews, more used to ground support operations of late, were schooled in single-engined flight, bomb-aiming, defensive manoeuvres, formation flying by day, instrument flying by night and night landings.

At Bialystok II./KG 4 had been appointed as the force's pathfinder unit, which entailed all crews attending a four-week course at the Luftwaffe's specialist school of navigation at Strausberg, near Berlin, to be taught the intricacies of celestial and radio-navigation.

Training was finally completed on 21 March 1944 and, although still officially listed under the *'Auffrischungsstab Ost'*, the *Gruppen* launched their long-awaited strategic air offensive against the enemy six days later. Most of their early targets were railway stations, whose names – Sarny, Kalinkovichi, Zhepetovka and Fastov – mean very little today, but back then were vital hubs in the Soviet rail supply network.

The exigencies of war soon intruded on Göring's grand plan, however. On 4 March the Red Army had unleashed its spring offensive, one result of which was the encirclement of a German force at Kovel, close to the

Offering a much more realistic picture of the third winter of the war on the Russian front are these rather tatty white Heinkels of I./KG 27

southern edge of the Pripyat Marshes. In response to this latest Russian advance, Hitler had peremptorily ordered that a number of the towns and cities in its path should become *feste Plätze* ('fortified places') to be held at all costs. Kovel was one of these 'fortified places', and the Heinkels of KG 55 were given the responsibility of keeping it supplied by air.

It was hardly the kind of operation for which the crews had just undergone four months of intensive training, but they answered the call nonetheless. In the eight days from 31 March to 7 April – and in the face of fierce enemy opposition – they flew a total of 221 missions, dropping almost 275,000 kilograms of supplies into Kovel. At night the aircraft were sent in individually at carefully timed two-minute intervals, releasing their loads at low level over a dropping zone marked by 'six bright lanterns'. By day they flew in close formation – their only means of defence against the overwhelming numbers of Soviet fighters. Their performance was acknowledged by a tongue-in-cheek passage in a report written some time later by the Waffen-SS commander of the Kovel 'fortress', *Obergruppenführer* (Generalleutnant) Herbert Gille;

'The accuracy with which the Luftwaffe, despite the heavy flak both by day and night, dropped its supply bombs into such a very confined area was admirable. I *was* rudely awoken once, however. That was when a supply bomb whose parachute had failed to open landed in my room. But apart from a hole in the wall and a few sticks of furniture demolished, there was, thank God, no other damage!'

On 11 May I. and II./KG 55 were transferred down to Focsani, in Rumania, for five days to help cover the evacuation by sea of the last German troops still fighting on the Crimea. Such diversions aside, Göring was still determined to establish his strategic bomber force in Poland. By this time the all-too-transparent 'Auffrischungsstab Ost' had been dispensed with and IV. *Fliegerkorps* had reverted to its proper title. Before May was out the *Korps* had been reinforced by two additional Heinkel *Kampfgruppen*, with I./KG 27 and I./KG 53 taking up residence at Baranovichi and Radom, respectively.

By mid-June three further *Gruppen* – III./KG 27 and II. and III./KG 53 – had also been added to the *Korps'* strength. Excluding its reconnaissance elements, IV. *Fliegerkorps* was now an all-Heinkel force, made up of ten *Kampfgruppen* totalling on average more than 250 serviceable machines. And it was about to carry out one of the single most successful strategic bombing raids ever to be mounted by the He 111 on the eastern front – which, ironically, would be directed against the USAAF's Eighth Air Force!

By mid-1944 Germany had moved as much of its industrial production as possible to the easternmost reaches of the Reich in order to preserve it from the growing threat of the USAAF daylight bomber offensive. America's answer had been to try to reach an agreement with the Soviet authorities that would allow its four-engined bombers – accompanied by their long-range escort fighters – to take off from their bases in the west, attack a target in eastern Germany and then land on a Russian airfield to refuel and re-arm. Several days later the USAAF aircraft would make the return trip to England, again bombing Germany on the way home.

The Soviet regime had somewhat grudgingly acceded to the American proposal and had prepared and enlarged four airfields in the newly liberated Ukraine to accommodate their Western Allies during their temporary stopovers. The first so-called 'shuttle' mission had in fact been flown on 2 June by 130 B-17s of the USAAF's Fifteenth Air Force based in Italy. After bombing the marshalling yards at Debreczen, in Hungary, this force had continued on eastwards to land at Poltava and Mirgorod, two of the Soviet airbases roughly midway between Kiev and Kharkov that had been made available to them. Four days later the Flying Fortresses took off again, bombing a Rumanian airfield on their way back to Italy.

This operation had come as a complete surprise to the Germans, who immediately began to consider what countermeasures could be taken. And what better way to combat the enemy's strategic bombing offensive than by using the Luftwaffe's own strategic bomber force? It was obvious that the best chance of putting a stop to such shuttle missions would be for the Heinkels of IV. *Fliegerkorps* to inflict 'one devastating blow against the American air fleet while it was on the ground in the Soviet Union'.

For most of the first three weeks of June 1944 the American 'heavies' had focussed their activities on northwest Europe in support of the Normandy invasion. Then, on 21 June, more than 1300 four-engined bombers of the Eighth Air Force began taking off from their bases in eastern England to attack targets in Germany. The great majority were heading for Berlin, but a smaller formation of 163 B-17s flew on to attack the hydrogenation plant at Ruhland, some 140 kilometres to the south-southeast of the German capital. Having done so, it did not follow the main force back towards the North Sea and home, but set course eastwards. It was the moment the Luftwaffe's trackers had been waiting and watching for.

IV. *Fliegerkorps* HQ at Brest-Litovsk was alerted even before the American bombers had crossed the frontline in the east into Soviet-held territory. While a 'shadowing' He 177 long-range reconnaissance aircraft of 2.(F)/100 continued to monitor the enemy's progress, the *Korps* began to implement the plans already put in place for this very eventuality. By the early afternoon of 21 June, even though the Americans' exact destination was not yet known, preparations for the mission were already well underway. At 1500 hrs the *Korps* finally received the signal informing them of their targets;

'Airfields Poltava and Mirgorod to be attacked tonight. Purpose of raids – to destroy US bombers and fighters simultaneously.'

The bespectacled Oberleutnant Dietrich Kornblum, *Staffelkapitän* of 4./KG 53, is shown here proudly wearing the Knight's Cross newly awarded to him on 9 June 1944. Two further points of interest are the 500 kg bomb filled with the highly explosive *Trialen*-mixture just behind Kornblum and those distinctly camouflaged He 111s in the background. Would 'KM' be one of the aircraft attacking Poltava in less than two weeks' time?

He 111s of KG 55 lined up at Deblin on the evening of 21 June 1944, awaiting the order to take off. Although scheduled to bomb Mirgorod, they would follow the Heinkels of KG 53 to Poltava instead

Final plans could now be made. Within the hour IV. *Fliegerkorps* had sent out orders to its subordinate units;

'KGs 27 and 53, with II./KG 4 as pathfinder *Gruppe*, to attack airfield Poltava. I. KG 55, with III./KG 4 as pathfinder *Gruppe*, to attack airfield Mirgorod.'

Because of the distances involved, the aircraft of KGs 27 and 53 had to be moved up from their present bases around Brest-Litovsk and Radom to more forward fields in the Bialystok and Minsk areas. Here, they were topped up with fuel, and those machines already bombed up for the night's intended attacks on the Soviet rail network had to be reloaded with a mix of SC 50s fitted with non-delay fuses, fragmentation bombs and incendiaries.

The timing of the raid was crucial as the He 111s had only a three-and-a-half hour window of darkness – from 2230 hrs on 21 June until 0200 hrs the following morning – for the flight over enemy territory. The bombing was therefore set to begin at midnight, which would allow all *Gruppen* to be back across the frontlines before first light on 22 June.

The first pathfinders of KG 4 began taking off from Baranovichi at 2030 hrs;

'It was still light as our heavy birds, getting on in age but still willing, started to roll. Kicking up huge columns of dust behind them, they trundled across the sandy surface of the field, slowly gathering speed until lifting off into an evening sky full of menacing black thunderclouds.'

However, the carefully planned operation was already beginning to unravel. At Puchovichi and Pinsk-West KG 27 failed to get off the ground. Many reference sources have since blamed this on a sudden torrential cloudburst, which turned the fields' grass surfaces into lakes of mud and prevented the heavily loaded Heinkels from getting airborne, but members of the *Geschwader* flatly deny this. There *was* no such sudden downpour at either field (which were, in any case, a good 200 kilometres apart) they maintain.

The actual reason for their failure to take off lay in the fact that the maximum range of the He 111H-20 – the variant of the Heinkel bomber with which KG 27 was fully equipped – was a good 600 kilometres less than that of the earlier H-16 model flown by the bulk of the other units (II./KG 4 had a few H-20s on strength, but these were not used during the mission). This meant that KG 27's jumping off points had to be as close to the front as possible. Many of their aircraft did not reach these forward fields until 2000 hrs – just 30 minutes before the operation was scheduled to commence. There simply was not time enough to refuel and bomb up the machines and brief the crews!

At a stroke the attacking force had been reduced by a third. Now KG 53 would target the Flying Fortresses at Poltava alone, leaving KG 55 to attack Mirgorod, where the Americans' escorting P-51 fighters had put down.

Those already aloft were having their troubles too. Five of II./KG 4's aircraft had to abort while *en route* to Poltava – two of the target markers, one target illuminator, one course indicator and one initial point marker. The remainder plunged on through the thickening cloud. Lightning flashed and St Elmo's fire transformed each machine's propellers into 'twin rings of iridescent blue-white fire'. The air was full of static electricity, making radio-navigation almost impossible. Relying on dead-reckoning alone, the leading aircraft flew over the unseen frontlines. At 2240 hrs a barrage of flak off to port confirmed that they were over enemy territory. Then, shortly after crossing the Dnieper north of Kiev, the clouds began to break up. Soon the night sky was a 'glittering canopy of stars'.

II./KG 4's first green marker went down to the right of Poltava's short east-west runway

Flying at a height of 3500 metres in the van of the Poltava force, Major Reinhard Graubner, the *Gruppenkommandeur* of the pathfinders of II./KG 4, was responsible for directing the attack on the American B-17s. He had been appointed *1. Steuermann* (literally '1st Helmsman', roughly the equivalent of the RAF Bomber Command's 'Master of Ceremonies' – much of the *'Auffrischungsstab Ost's'* recent training had been based on the Luftwaffe's acquired knowledge of British night bombing procedures). Now Graubner was anxiously scanning the skies ahead for any evidence of activity.

At 2315 hrs he saw the moving fingers of searchlights. Poltava or Mirgorod? They were still too far away to tell. The minutes ticked by. The first flares were due to go down over Mirgorod at 2340 hrs, but there was no sign of them. Major Graubner began to feel uneasy. Should he sacrifice some height to gain a fix on the ground? He resisted the temptation. At 2343 hrs a flare exploded into brilliance directly ahead of him. As it slowly floated earthwards he heard a voice in his earphones – '*Indianer* to *Kapitän 1* – target identified!' It was one of his own crews, and they had found Poltava.

Having done so, albeit nearly ten minutes ahead of schedule, they had quickly released a flare for fear of losing sight of it again. Other crews added several more flares to the first. The Poltava flak then opened up and searchlights began to probe the night sky for the raiders overhead. In the growing brightness two runways became visible. Alongside them, long rows of four-engined aircraft gleamed a dull silver against the dark earth.

Graubner wasted no more time. At 2355 hrs he ordered *'Fackelzug'* ('Torchlight Procession'). Dozens more flares started to rain down. Poltava was lit

The attack in progress as seen from the air...

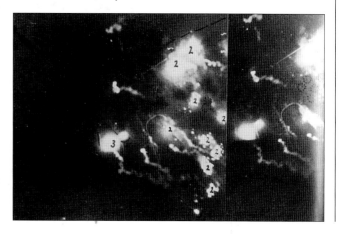

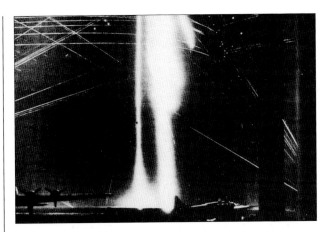

. . . and from the ground

up as bright as day. Next came the voice of the leading ground marker. 'Dropping green candy in three minutes!' Graubner waited for the marker to fall, noting its exact position before pressing his microphone. 'Green candy location eastern end of short runway!' Then it was the turn of the sole target marker to reach Poltava. He placed his bright red marker flare precisely in the centre of the runway cross. Now the bombing could begin.

Hearing Graubner's 'Bomb on the red marker!', Oberstleutnant Fritz Pockrandt, the *Geschwaderkommodore* of KG 53, led his crews in to the attack. Moments later hundreds of small one- and two-kilogram fragmentation bombs were cutting broad flickering swathes across the surface of the field. Among them could be seen the shuddering blossoms of heavier bombs exploding. After a few minutes a large fire was blazing. 'Fire is on the western edge of the field', Graubner radioed as he continued to circle above Poltava, giving directions to the incoming Heinkels of KG 53, praising the accuracy of some, chiding others.

Bombs were still falling almost without pause, one stick hard on the heels of the last – sometimes three or four sticks all at the same time – when Graubner noticed yet more flares being added to the inferno below. He wondered briefly where they were coming from. In fact, they were coming from the pathfinders of III./KG 4, and were the result of the final mishap of the night – a mishap that was to seal the fate of yet more of the Flying Fortresses at Poltava. The Mirgorod force, which had been scheduled to open the attack, was several minutes late in approaching its

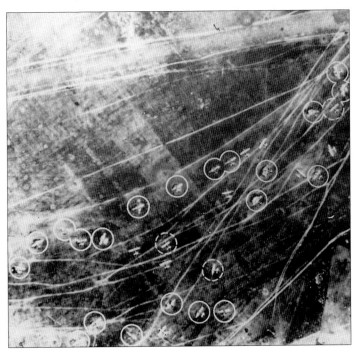

Photo analysis of the results of the raid on Poltava. No fewer than 44 American B-17s were destroyed and a further 26 damaged – almost exactly half the number of bombers that had attacked the Ruhland hydrogenation plant before heading east to land in Russia

target. As it did so, many of III./KG 4's crews spotted the premature flares going down over Poltava some 80 kilometres to the northwest. Wrongly assuming that these flares marked the start of the attack on Mirgorod, they turned in that direction.

When Oberstleutnant Wilhelm Antrup, the *Geschwaderkommodore* of KG 55, realised what was happening and discovered that there were now too few pathfinders ahead of him to illuminate Mirgorod properly, he very sensibly ordered his crews to attack Poltava too. He was unable to inform Major Graubner of his decision, however, as the two forces were on different radio frequencies.

Gradually, the thick smoke from the many flares burning out on the ground, mixed with that of the fires from blazing aircraft and fuel dumps, began to shroud the airfield. Targets were becoming harder to identify. The final bombs were being dropped almost at random and causing little additional damage. At 0020 hrs Graubner was heard calling KG 53's Oberstleutnant Pockrandt suggesting that the attack be terminated. The latter agreed and Graubner issued his final order of the night, the single codeword *'Feierabend!'* – 'Closing time!'

As the last of the Heinkels turned away, the occasional explosion still rocked Poltava and 15 large fires were burning unchecked on the field. Behind them the raiders left the wreckage of 44 B-17s and 15 other American and Soviet aircraft totally destroyed, plus 26 further B-17s damaged. Not one Heinkel was lost.

Unlike many Luftwaffe units of World War 2, the He 111 *Kampfgeschwader* on the Russian front had thus ended *their* war with a bang, not a whimper. For within two hours of their landing back on their bases in Poland, the Red Army had launched the great 1944 summer offensive that heralded the start of its drive to the German border and, ultimately, to Berlin. In a desperate attempt to halt the offensive in its tracks, IV. *Fliegerkorps'* Heinkels were immediately returned to the ground-

KG 53 was withdrawn from the Russian front on 17 August 1944 and sent to eastern France to fly night supply missions to pockets of German troops cut off in Normandy. Within days it had suffered crippling losses, among them 3. *Staffel's* 'A1+AL', which is seen here being inspected by US soldiers. Note the glider-towing attachment in the machine's tail

support role. But the more numerous Fw 190-equipped *Schlachtgruppen* were obviously better suited to this task, and also stood a much greater chance of survival in skies now dominated by the Red Air Force. Although the He 111s did carry out a few more nocturnal strategic raids after Poltava, mainly against rail targets, their days as a viable fighting force in the east were over.

On 12 August KG 55, now back on German soil, flew its final eastern front bombing mission when it attacked the Vistula bridges around Warsaw. After a brief spell then spent carrying out transport duties in the west, the *Geschwader* was withdrawn from operations in September to commence retraining as a single-engined fighter unit under the designation KG(J) 55. The three *Gruppen* of KG 27 were to follow suit in October when they left their bases in East Prussia to begin converting to Bf 109s and Fw 190s in Austria as KG(J) 27.

The only units to escape redesignation were the *Geschwaders'* two semi-autonomous, specialised anti-railway *Staffeln*, 14.(*Eis.*)/KG 27 and 14.(*Eis.*)/KG 55, the latter having been created in June 1943 by the redesignation of 9./KG 53. Rarely more than a dozen aircraft strong – and frequently reduced to as few as three or four serviceable machines each – they were to continue their train-busting activities throughout 1944 and into 1945, the former under *Luftflotte* 4 in the south and the latter under *Luftflotte* 1 (and subsequently *Luftflotte* 6) to the north.

In August 1944 KG 53 had also been withdrawn from the eastern front, initially to participate in the defence of Normandy, but then to undergo training as V1 carriers for a series of air-launched flying-bomb attacks on England.

With three of its four component *Geschwader* transferred elsewhere, IV. *Fliegerkorps* was finally disbanded in September 1944, leaving just the

The only Heinkel bombers remaining in the east during the winter of 1944-45 were those of KG 4. These late war He 111H-20s, which were fitted with a turret in place of the earlier variants' dorsal gun positions, are believed to be aircraft of II./KG 4, with the *Gruppenstab's* 'DC' in the foreground

Heinkels of KG 4 operational in the east. This *Geschwader* had recently been caught up in the fighting in Rumania, brought about by that country's prompt change of sides upon the approach of the Red Army. KG 4 lost at least two of its machines to Rumanian-flown Bf 109s, and had carried out a bombing raid on the famous Ploesti oilfields – now occupied by the Russians – before being called upon to assist in the evacuation of German forces from Rumania. The Heinkels carried up to 12 passengers a time on each of their airlift missions across the Carpathians back into Hungary.

And it was in Hungary, now under I. *Fliegerkorps*, that KG 4 would spend much of the remainder of the year. Few operations were flown during this period, but at the end of September a reinforced 2. *Staffel was* sent south to take part in the evacuation of the German garrisons from the Aegean Islands. Based at Salonika-Sedes and shuttling nightly from there to Crete, Athens and back, it proved a perilous undertaking. The *Staffel* lost eight of its 15 aircraft in the space of just ten days. A similar deployment to the Balkans by elements of II. *Gruppe* in mid-October was equally costly – four machines were written-off in one night alone while trying to land at Agram (Zagreb) in bad weather.

By the second half of October, with the sixth and last winter of the war already beginning to tighten its grip, all three *Gruppen* of KG 4 were based at Papa in northwest Hungary, little more than 60 kilometres from the Austrian border. There they fielded a considerable force of 78 Heinkels, 52 of which were currently serviceable. But by this stage of the hostilities numbers alone were no longer a measure of operational effectiveness. A combination of ever worsening weather and – more critically – a growing shortage of fuel kept the *Geschwader's* aircraft firmly anchored to the ground for most of the time.

Also fitted with a mid-upper turret, this 6. *Staffel* machine (letter 'P' just discernible on original print) sports an entirely different camouflage scheme from the aircraft in the previous photograph, and may well belong to a transport unit. Note the three tiny dots ahead of the fuselage cross – some sources suggest these are small signal lights (green, red and white) associated with the dropping of supplies by night

The Red Army, however, was paying little heed either to the weather conditions or to its enemy's dire lack of fuel. Continuing their inexorable advance westwards, Soviet forces surrounded the Hungarian capital Budapest on 26 December. The Luftwaffe was tasked with mounting yet another airlift to keep the 70,000 encircled German and Hungarian troops supplied. A scratch force of Ju 52/3m and Do 17 transport units was hastily assembled, to which were added the Heinkels of I. and II./KG 4 (III. *Gruppe* being on temporary deployment to Poland).

With the shorter-range Ju 52/3ms requiring the use of Papa, I. and II./KG 4 moved out to Novy Dvor, in Slovakia, and Wiener Neustadt, respectively. The weather was appalling. During one 48-hour period in mid-January nearly a metre of snow fell on Wiener Neustadt and a 30-metre wide, over 800-metre long takeoff strip – some 25,000 cubic metres of snow in all – had to be shovelled free by hand! Despite such difficulties, the crews of KG 4 (III. *Gruppe* having joined II./KG 4 at Wiener Neustadt at the beginning of January 1945) were sometimes able to fly up to three missions a night into Budapest.

But their efforts were to prove of little help. The Hungarian capital could not be saved. As in so many similar situations before it, a relief attempt – on this occasion by IV. SS-*Panzerkorps* – was unable to fight its way through. Budapest fell on 11 February. Last-minute permission had been given to attempt a breakout, and during the nights of 14 and 15 February nine He 111s of KG 4 dropped supplies to scattered ground units hiding in woods to the west of Budapest. Less than 800 men were later to reach the by now dubious safety of the German lines.

For no sooner had one crisis run its inevitable course than another loomed – this time around the 'fortress' city of Breslau on the River Oder, which had been surrounded by the Russians on 15 February. The miscellany of units holding Breslau had more than 200 artillery pieces, seven tanks and eight self-propelled guns in their armoury, but they were desperately short of ammunition. The transport *Gruppen* that had been engaged in supplying Budapest immediately began dropping munitions of all kinds into Breslau. KG 4 took the risk of flying its first missions in close formation during the hours of daylight. And the risk appeared to be paying off, as its He 111s covered the 350 kilometres to Breslau without loss – only to have two of their number then shot down by the city's flak defences. It transpired that the gunners, unused to seeing so many aircraft in the air all at once, had opened fire 'just to be on the safe side!'

Not surprisingly perhaps, subsequent operations were flown under the cover of darkness. When Novy Dvor and Wiener Neustadt came under threat from the advancing Red Army, I. and III./KG 4 transferred to Dresden-Klotzsche and Wels, in Upper Austria, with two machines falling victim to prowling US fighters on the way. In March III. *Gruppe* then moved to Königgrätz (Hradec Králové), in the Protectorate of Bohemia, where it was joined by I./KG 4 towards the end of April. It was to be the final move of the war for both *Gruppen*, as the end was now only days away.

The two *Gruppens'* last supply missions to Breslau were flown on the night of 26/27 April when 30 of their aircraft dropped more than 24 tons of ammunition to the city's defenders. But it was no use. Soviet forces captured the 'fortress' of Breslau nine days later.

At Königgrätz, the subsequent fortunes of I. and III./KG 4 would prove to be very different. Packed with groundcrews and other personnel, the Heinkels of I. *Gruppe* were allowed to take off and head west for destinations of their own choosing in those parts of the Reich not yet occupied by the victorious Allies. But, for some unknown reason, the crews of III./KG 4 were ordered to drain the tanks of their machines (the fuel being passed to the ground-attack Fw 190s of SG 4) and then blow their aircraft up. Forced to strike west on roads jammed solid with refugees fleeing from the Russians, many members of the *Gruppe* were subsequently caught and taken into Soviet captivity.

The personnel of II./KG 4 also ended up as prisoners-of-war – of the British. At the beginning of March this *Gruppe* had been transferred from Wiener Neustadt up into central Germany. Based at Pretzsch, on the River Elbe (little more than 20 kilometres from the spot where American and Soviet troops would link hands the following month), II./KG 4 was subordinated to the *Gefechtsverband* (Battle Group) Helbig, the force tasked with preventing the Soviets from advancing across the River Oder. The *Gruppe* was to fly several missions against the Oder bridges, operating as pathfinders and 'illuminators' for the Ju 88/Bf 109 *Mistel* combinations of II./KG 200, as well as for some of the attacks carried out by single-engined suicide units, whose pilots had pledged to crash their aircraft into the bridges. By April II./KG 4's Heinkels had been moved further north to Anklam and Greifswald, on the Baltic Coast.

It was from here that crews undertook their final operations of the war, dropping supplies into the last and greatest eastern front 'fortress' of them all – Berlin. By the time the late *Führer's* capital surrendered on 2 May 1945, II./KG 4 had retired to Grossenbrode. And from there it was not much more than a 100-kilometre hop to Eggebek in Schleswig-Holstein and British captivity.

III./KG 4's war in the east ended at Königgrätz (Hradec Králové) in the then Protectorate of Bohemia, where this sorry-looking quartet of He 111s was photographed after the German surrender

APPENDICES

REPRESENTATIVE HE 111 BOMBER STRENGTHS

A) JUNE 1941, *BARBAROSSA*

		Base	Est-Serv
Luftflotte 1 (North)			
Stab KG 1	Oberst Karl Angerstein	Powunden	1-1
Luftflotte 2 (Centre)			
Stab KG 53	Obstlt Paul Weitkus	Radom	6-4
I./KG 53	Obstlt Erich Kaufmann	Grojec	28-18
II./KG 53	Maj Hans Steinweg	Radom	20-10
III./KG 53	Maj Richard Fabian	Radzyn	31-22
Luftflotte 4 (South)			
Stab KG 27	Maj Gerhard Ulbricht	Focsani-South	5-5
I./KG 27	Hptm (?) Reinhard	Focsani-South	30-22
II./KG 27	Hptm Reinhard Günzel	Focsani-South	24-21
III./KG 27	Hptm Hans-Henning *Frhr* von Beust	Zilistea	28-25
II./KG 4	Maj Wolfgang Bühring	Zilistea	24-8
Stab KG 55	Obstlt Benno Kosch	Labunie	6-6
I./KG 55	Hptm Rudolf Kiel	Labunie	27-27
II./KG 55	Maj *Dr* Ernst Kühl	Labunie	24-22
III./KG 55	Hptm Heinrich Wittmer	Klemensov	25-24
Total			**279-215**

B) JULY 1942, BLAU/BRAUNSCHWEIG

		Base	Est-Serv
Luftflotte 5 (Arctic)			
I./KG 26	Hptm Bert Eicke (acting)	Bardufoss	29-24
Luftflotte 1 (North)			
Stab KG 53	Oberst Paul Weitkus	Gostkino?	4-4
I./KG 53	Maj Fritz Pockrandt	Gostkino?	31-23
Lw Kdo Ost (Centre)			
Stab KG 4	Obstlt *Dr* Gottlieb Wolff	Sechinskaya	3-3
I./KG 4	Hptm Helmuth Boltze	Sechinskaya	26-23
II./KG 4	Maj Rolf von Samson-Himmelstjerna	Smolensk-North	25-19
II./KG 53	Obstlt Schulz-Müllensiefen	Shatalovk	33-26
Luftflotte 4 (South)			
Stab KG 27	Maj Hans-Henning *Frhr* von Beust	Kursk	2-2
I./KG 27	Hptm Rudolf Müller	Poltava	32-20
II./KG 27	Maj Reinhard Günzel	Kursk	31-21
III./KG 27	?	Kursk	31-8
Stab KG 55	Oberst Benno Kosch	Kramatorskaya	4-4
I./KG 55	Maj Rudolf Kiel	Kutelnikovo	31-19
II./KG 55	Obstlt *Dr* Ernst Kühl	Kramatorskaya	30-21
III./KG 55	Obstlt Hermann *Frhr* von dem Bongart	Kramatorskaya	29-20
Stab KG 100	Obstlt Heinz-Ludwig von Holleben	Saki	1-1
I./KG 100	Maj Werner Hoffmann	Saki	37-13
III./KG 4	Hptm Hermann Kühl	Nikolayen-East	35-18
Total			**414-269**

C) JULY 1943, *ZITADELLE*

Luftflotte 6 (Centre)

Stab KG 4	Maj Werner Klosinski	Karachev	2-2
II./KG 4	Maj Reinhard Graubner	Sechinskaya	34-24
III./KG 4	Maj Kurt Neumann	Karachev	38-29
Stab KG 53	Obstlt Fritz Pockrandt	Bryansk	2-2
I./KG 53	Maj Karl Rauer	Sechinskaya	33-23
III./KG 53	Maj Emil Allmendinger	Bryansk	16-15

Luftflotte 4 (South)

Stab KG 27	Obstlt Hans-Henning *Frhr* von Beust	Dnepropetrovsk	2-1
I./KG 27	Maj Joachim Petzold	Zaporozhye	20-14
II./KG 27	Maj Karl-August Petersen	Dnepropetrovsk	32-21
III./KG 27	Hptm Heinrich Klein	Dnepropetrovsk	32-24
14.(*Eis.*)/KG 27	Olt Eduard Skrzipek	?	11-8
Stab KG 55	Oberst Benno Kosch	Kharkov/Rogan	5-4
II./KG 55	Maj Walter Traub	Kharkov-East	32-21
III./KG 55	Maj Wilhelm Antrup	Stalino	43-38
I./KG 100	Maj Hansgeorg Bätcher	Poltava	11-8

Total   **313-234**

D) JUNE 1944, POLTAVA

Luftflotte 1 (North)

14.(*Eis.*)/KG 55	Olt Mathias Bermadinger	Jakobstadt	9-4

Luftflotte 6 (Centre)

Stab KG 4	Obstlt Werner Klosinski	Bialystok	8-6
II./KG 4	Maj Reinhard Graubner	Baranovichi	34-30
III./KG 4	Maj Ernst-Dieter von Tellemann	Bialystok	40-27
Stab KG 27	?	Krosno	1-0
I./KG 27	Hptm Horst Quednau	Krosno	41-28
III./KG 27	Hptm Heinrich Klein	Mielec	35-6
Stab KG 53	Obstlt Fritz Pockrandt	Radom	1-1
I./KG 53	Maj Karl Rauer	Radom	36-30
II./KG 53	Maj Herbert Wittmann	Piastov	37-18
III./KG 53	Maj Emil Allmendinger	Radom	36-35
Stab KG 55	Obstlt Wilhelm Antrup	Deblin-Irena	1-1
I./KG 55	Maj Richard Brunner	Deblin-Ulez	35-31
II./KG 55	Maj Heinz Höfer	Deblin-Irena	35-27
III./KG 55	Maj Alfred Bollmann	Grojec	36-35

Luftflotte 4 (South)

I./KG 4	Hptm Ernst Göpel	Focsani	43-27
14.(*Eis.*)/KG 27	Hptm Eduard Skrzipek	Krosno	14-9

Total   **442-315**

E) APRIL 1945, END

Luftflotte Reich (North)

II./KG 4	Maj Carl-Otto Hesse	Greifswald	21-21

Luftflotte 6 (South)

Stab KG 4	Maj Reinhard Graubner	Königgrätz	1-1
I./KG 4	Hptm Rolf Rannersmann	Königgrätz	24-21
III./KG 4	Maj Herbert von Kruska	Königgrätz	27-24
7./KG 53	Hptm Kurt Bausek	Alt-Lönnewitz	5-2

Total   **78-69**

COLOUR PLATES

1
He 111H '5J+GN' of 5./KG 4 'General Wever', Koroye Selo, December 1941
Although all eastern front He 111s embarked upon *Barbarossa* in standard dark green/black-green temperate finish, the Russian winter soon forced them to adopt some appropriate form of camouflage. Obviously just back from II./KG 4's ten-week period of rest and refit in East Prussia, 5. *Staffel*'s 'GN' displays a pristine coat of white paint – it would not stay that way for long!

2
He 111H '5J+HT' of 9./KG 4 'General Wever', Königsberg-Prowehren, June 1942
During the three weeks of Operation *Froschlaich* ('Frogspawn') – the mining of the main Soviet naval base at Kronstadt – the machines of KG 4, heavily loaded with two aerial mines apiece, had to use jettisonable underwing rocket packs in order to get off the ground for the long 830-kilometre haul from East Prussia to the target area. Its undersides painted black, 9. *Staffel*'s 'HT' is pictured here with both mines and rocket packs at the start of one such mission.

3
He 111H-6 '5J+HR' of 7./KG 4 'General Wever', Smolensk-North, December 1942
Sporting a distinctly 'war-weary' overall white finish during the depths of the second winter on the Russian front, '5J+HR' was one of the 165 He 111s that would be reported lost, missing or damaged beyond repair during the Stalingrad airlift. It came to grief while attempting to land inside the pocket on 17 January 1943. Fortunately, Leutnant Spannbauer and his crew survived to be flown out by a machine of KG 55 the following day.

4
He 111 '5J+LN' of 5./KG 4 'General Wever', Orel-West, June 1943
Anonymous under its all-enveloping coat of temporary black distemper, except for the small 'last two' in white high on the rear fuselage, 'LN' of 5./KG 4 displays a typical finish applied to the Heinkels participating in the night raids on Gorki and other strategic targets in the run-up to *Zitadelle*.

5
He 111H-20 '5J+CT' of 9./KG 4 'General Wever', Königgrätz, March 1945
Wearing what can only be described as a rather exuberant pattern of 'patches and lines' over its basic camouflage finish, possibly prompted by the patchwork nature of the ground during the spring thaw of 1945, 'CT' was one of the machines taking part in the Breslau airlift during the closing weeks of the war.

6
He 111H-20 '5J+AH' of 1./KG 4 'General Wever', Königgrätz, April 1945
This densely polka-dotted H-20 of 1./KG 4 also took part in the Budapest and Breslau air supply drops of early 1945. Like most of 1. *Staffel*'s machines, it ended up crash-landing 'somewhere in the west' at the close of the war. Bearing the individual

aircraft letter 'A', the He 111 may have been the mount of *Staffelkapitän* Hauptmann Dietrich Grassmann, one of the last of KG 4's 27 eastern front Knight's Cross winners.

7
He 111H-20 '5J+CT' of 9./KG 4 'General Wever', Königgrätz, May 1945
Another highly individualistic camouflage scheme as sported by KG 4 in the closing weeks of the war. Although III. *Gruppe* had been ordered to blow up its aircraft at Königgrätz, this particular machine – presumably a replacement for the earlier 'CT' depicted in profile 5 – apparently escaped the net (or its pilot simply disobeyed orders) for it too ended its career 'somewhere in the west' on its belly in a field surrounded by a group of curious American GIs.

8
He 111H-4 '1H+ML' of 3./KG 26 'Löwe', Kemi, August 1941
Wearing standard temperate camouflage colours, but with yellow theatre markings freshly added to indicate its recent arrival on the eastern font, 'ML' is believed to have been one of the first six aircraft of I./KG 26 transferred from Norway to Kemi, in Finland, in mid-August 1941 to fly bombing missions against the strategically important Murmansk railway. This *Gruppe* had previously been engaged on anti-shipping operations over the North Sea, as witness the tiny white silhouette of a ship (or submarine?) at the base of the rudder.

9
He 111H-6 '1H+AK' of 2./KG 26 'Löwe', Kalinin, December 1941
This aircraft poses something of a mystery. According to all known sources, KG 26, after spending several weeks in action against the Murmansk railway, was transferred up to Banak, in northern Norway, in the autumn of 1941 to bomb the Russian Arctic ports of Murmansk and Archangelsk, before then being sent to Italy early in 1942 to commence torpedo training. Nowhere is mention made of any of its aircraft being involved on the Moscow front. Yet this machine, clearly bearing the markings of 2. *Staffel* (and equipped with a grenade-launcher in the tail), was captured almost undamaged by the Russians after belly landing at Kalinin, some 170 kilometres to the northwest of the Soviet capital, on 17 December 1941.

10
He 111H-6 '1G+GP' of 6./KG 27 'Boelcke', Koroye Selo, March 1942
Wearing a precautionary coat of white distemper on its uppersurfaces thanks to Koroye Selo still being carpeted in snow in March 1942, this is possibly the 'GP' of 6./KG 27 that was shot down during a supply flight to Cholm on 7 April 1942.

11
He 111H-6 '1G+FL' of 3./KG 27 'Boelcke', Stalino, May 1942
Proving, if proof were needed, that even the Luftwaffe sometimes got it wrong, this machine was clearly intended

for service in the Mediterranean theatre and yet ended up with 3./KG 27 on the eastern front. Although it stood out like a sore thumb in any formation, Leutnant Harro Wooge and his crew grew attached to their 'FL'. Because its desert finish was very similar in colour to the brownshirts of Hitler's SA, it was known in the *Staffel* as the 'Nazi bomber'!

12
He 111H-6y '1G+CM' of 4./KG 27 'Boelcke', Kursk, September 1942
KG 27 was equipped almost entirely with H-6s throughout the whole of 1942, including several fitted with the *'Y-Gerät'* beam-guidance bombing device, as identified here by the prominent additional aerial forward of the dorsal gun position. Aircraft of this type were reportedly employed by the *Geschwader* during its first bombing raids on Stalingrad in the early autumn of that year. Note also the 20 mm MG FF cannon in the nose and ventral gondola.

13
He 111H-20 '1G+CH' of 1./KG 27 'Boelcke', Prosskurov, February 1944
Wearing a very tight scribble scheme over all uppersurfaces, 1. *Staffel's* 'CH' is depicted during the time the unit was heavily engaged in flying supplies into the Cherkassy/Korsun pocket, where two German *Korps* – some 56,000 men in all – had been surrounded during the Red Army's advance through the Ukraine. On this occasion, thanks in no small part to the Luftwaffe's airlift operations, more than half the encircled troops managed to break out after a three-week battle.

14
He 111H-20 '1G+FH'of 1./KG 27 'Boelcke', Baranovichi, May 1944
By the end of May 1944, having supported the German retreat across the Ukraine, I./KG 27 had moved up to Baranovichi to become part of IV. *Fliegerkorps'* strategic bomber force. Sporting a much more open 'scribble' than sister ship 'CH' immediately above, this machine of 1. *Staffel* has been given matt black undersides more suited to its long-range night raids on the enemy's rear area rail network.

15
He 111H-16 '1G+LY' of 14.(*Eis.*)/KG 27 'Boelcke', Kemenetz, November 1944
While I./KG 27's strategic bombing campaign against the Soviet railway system was short-lived, the anti-railway specialists of 14.(*Eis.*)/KG 27 spent their entire two-year operational career (from February 1943 to early 1945) flying train-busting missions deep behind enemy lines. Operating alone at night, this *Staffel's* aircraft wore a variety of appropriate nocturnal finishes, such as that shown here, and eschewed yellow theatre markings altogether. Each was heavily armed (including ventral gun packs), but the jury is still out as to whether the device shown here on the tail of 'LY' is a grenade-launcher or (as one source suggests) a glider tug attachment.

16
He 111 '1T+KX' of 1./KG 28, Central Sector, Autumn 1941
Even by Luftwaffe standards, the operational history of

KG 28 is extraordinarily complex. The *Geschwader's* various subordinate units underwent at least ten different re-designations between the years 1939 and 1942! It is apparent from official records that at the time this particular machine was shot down near Moscow in the autumn of 1941, I./KG 28 was between two stools as KGr.126 and III./KG 26. What is *not* clear, however, is why it should be wearing the markings of 13. *Staffel* – i.e. part of a V. *Gruppe*?

17
He 111H-6y 'A1+AH' of 1./KG 53 'Legion Condor', Shatalovka, November 1941
Whoever gave this *'Y-Gerät'*-equipped H-6 a coat of winter white on its uppersurfaces was careful not to obliterate the *Gruppe* badge behind the cockpit. At this relatively early stage of the campaign in the east – when such emblems were still on display – it was nearly always the *Kapitän* of a *Staffel* who flew individual letter 'A', which would make this machine the mount of Hauptmann Emil Allmendinger.

18
He 111H-6 'A1+HL' of 3./KG 53 'Legion Condor', Riga-Spilve, February 1942
Wearing a decidedly more elaborate, if more crudely applied, temporary winter finish (which has covered up the unit badge), 3. *Staffel's* 'HL' was one of the aircraft that took part in the Demyansk and Cholm airlift operations.

19
He 111H-6 'A1+HT' of 9./KG 53 'Legion Condor', Gostkino, September 1942
Despite the many and varied winter camouflage schemes depicted on these pages, it should be remembered that the Heinkels wore standard two-tone green finish throughout the summer months. Having spent almost the whole of the first half of 1942 re-equipping in France, III./KG 53 returned to the eastern front in August, being based briefly at Smolensk-North before moving up to Gostkino in September. Here, crews put their newly acquired Lotfe 7D bombsights to good use during their raids on Leningrad.

20
He 111H-6 'A1+NP' of 6./KG 53 'Legion Condor', Voroshilovgrad, January 1943
Back to full winter garb, as sported here by 6. *Staffel's* 'NP'. Unlike III./KG 53's lengthy sojourn in the west, II. *Gruppe's* return to Germany in December 1942 – intended to make good its recent heavy losses – was cut short by the unit's hasty recall to the eastern front in mid-January 1943 to participate in the closing stages of the Stalingrad airlift. Whatever replacements they may have received during their brief time at Greifswald did not last long. By the end of January II./KG 53 had been reduced to just ten crews and seven aircraft, only three of which were serviceable!

21
He 111H-16 'A1+HL' of 3./KG 53 'Legion Condor', Mielec, March 1944
Another winter, another winter camouflage scheme – and quite a wild one at that! How many hands have been at work smothering 3. *Staffel's* 'HL' in this mad mix of patches, scribbles and dots? By early 1944 all three *Gruppen* of KG 53 were based

together at Mielec, in southern Poland, engaged solely on transport duties – as witness the tailcone glider tug attachment seen here. It would not be many weeks, however...

22
He 111H-16 'A1+EP' of 6./KG 53 'Legion Condor', Piastov, June 1944

. . . before KG 53 became part of IV. *Fliegerkorps'* strategic night bombing force. No sign of elaborate paintwork now, just a business-like black, alleviated only by a small 'last two' in yellow high on the tailfin. It was in machines such as this that KG 53 flew to Poltava on the night of 21/22 June 1944.

23
He 111H-4 'G1+AS' of 8./KG 55 'Greif', Klemensov, June 1941

Still in Poland, but three years earlier to the day and back to the start of *Barbarossa*, 'AS', the machine flown by 8./KG 55's *Staffelkapitän*, Hauptmann Karl Knorr, is seen here resplendent in its new eastern front yellow theatre markings. Note also both the *Geschwader's* 'Griffon' badge behind the cockpit and 8. *Staffel's* own 'Three little fishes' emblem at the base of the rudder.

24
He 111H-6 'G1+BN' of 5./KG 55 'Greif', Dnepropetrovsk, June 1942

Another *Staffel* to display its emblem on the rudder of its machines was 5./KG 55, whose cartoon-like 'Red worm' is seen here adorning 'BN'. The campaign against the Soviet Union is now a year old and, although II./KG 55 has only recently returned from a five-month spell of rest and re-equipment in western France, its aircraft are showing the effects – gone is the pristine finish of 'AS' in the previous profile, and gone too is the *Geschwader* badge.

25
He 111H-16 'G1+DK' of 2./KG 55 'Greif', Sarabuz, December 1943

2. *Staffel's* 'DK' wears a striking 'wave'-pattern camouflage similar to that seen on a number of other I. and III. *Gruppen* machines based in the Crimea towards the end of 1943. It was perhaps an 'all-purpose' scheme designed to suit the units' many operations over both land and water at that time, ranging from anti-partisan sweeps and heavy bombing missions to shipping escort duties.

26
He 111H-16 'G1+JT' of 9./KG 55 'Greif', Deblin-Irena, April 1944

A very neatly polka-dotted machine of 9./KG 55, depicted here at the end of its training as part of Göring's eastern front strategic bomber force. Oddly, April 1944 was the only month in which the five original He 111 *Kampfgruppen* of this force

were officially listed on the Luftwaffe's Order of Battle strength returns under the heading of *'Auffrischungsstab Ost'*, rather than IV. *Fliegerkorps*.

27
He 111H-16 'G1+LH' of 1./KG 55 'Greif', Deblin-Ulez, May 1944

Even as late as May 1944, many of the Heinkels of IV. *Fliegerkorps'* strategic strike force were still wearing the 'temporary' winter camouflage schemes they had adopted during their earlier training. 1./KG 55 seemed to favour variations on a disruptive pattern of hard-edged white (and darker green) patches, such as that sported here by 'LH'.

28
He 111H-16 'G1+DY' of 14.(*Eis.*)/KG 55 'Greif', Königsberg-Gutenfeld, October 1944

Like 14.(*Eis.*)/KG 27 (see profile 15), the train-busting 14.(*Eis.*)/KG 55 long outlived its parent *Geschwader's* withdrawal from operations for conversion to single-engined fighters. First formed (from 9./KG 55) in June 1943, the *Staffel* was not disbanded until the last week in April 1945. Unlike 14.(*Eis.*)/KG 27, however, it appeared not to favour special camouflage schemes. If 'DY' is anything to go by, the only concessions to the unit's nocturnal sorties were black undersides and flame dampers on the exhausts – although most aircraft did pack a powerful punch of anything up to six forward-firing 20 mm cannon.

29
He 111H-3 '6N+BL' of 3./KGr.100, Bobruisk, August 1941

In the final few hectic days at Chartres, in France, before the unit's hurried transfer to the Moscow front, the highly secret 'X-Gerät' radio beam navigation equipment was removed from all of KGr.100's Heinkels. But clearly there had not been time to remove the three prominent dorsal aerials, which gave the machines their nickname of *'Dreimaster'* ('Three-masters'). They would disappear over time, but many aircraft were still fitted with these now useless appendages during their early raids on the Soviet capital.

30
He 111H-6 '6N+IH' of 1./KG 100 'Wiking', Morosovskaya, November 1942

When, after two months spent re-equipping in the Reich, the unit returned to the southern sector of the Russian front in early 1942 as I. of the newly established KG 100 'Wiking', there was not a 'Three-master' to be seen. I./KG 100 continued to plough its own furrow, however. For some reason, it was the only Heinkel *Kampfgruppe* on the eastern front that was known to position its yellow theatre band partially *behind* the fuselage cross – a gift, or so it would seem, for any astute Soviet intelligence officer!

INDEX

References to illustrations are shown in **bold**. Plates are shown with page and caption locators in brackets.